Bristol Radical Par

C000262150

Hartcliffe Betrayed

The fading of a post-war dream

Paul Smith

ISBN 978-1-911522-74-4

Bristol Radical History Group. 2024.
www.brh.org.uk
brh@brh.org.uk

Contents

Introduction—1

1. Homes after the war—3

2. The battles for the Dundry Slopes—15

3. The grand plan—25

4. Building on the cheap—43

5. Building the community—65

6. Retail, education and other infrastructure—95

Conclusion—125

Appendices—131

Sources and Bibliography—141

Picture credits—143

Acknowledgements—144

"As much work has gone into Dundry as in the planning of satellite towns in other parts of the country and when finally the garden city arises it will be a venture of which Bristol will be justly proud." *Western Daily Press.*[1]

"A new estate is being built on the slopes of Dundry Hills. These were the 'dream places' of the well-to-do in days gone by. Labour took the view that they should be the 'living places' of the working people." *Alderman W H Hennessy.*[2]

"Almost every big mistake which can be made in the design of a housing estate was made at Hartcliffe ... In 1960, when the population was already 16,000 there were just six professionally qualified people living at Hartcliffe. I don't suppose the proportion is very different now, for who would choose to live there." *Bristol architect, Michael Jenner.*[3]

"This was the trouble in the beginning. Everybody sort of said Hartcliffe and turned their noses up ... It was the greatest mistake the corporation ever done when they just built the houses, with no roads and no facilities at all. There was no church, no shops." *Local resident, Jean Carey.*[4]

"It was beautiful though; it was like living in the middle of the country." *Local resident, Pamela Winchester.*[5]

1   *Western Daily Press*, 24 January 1950.
2   *Bristol Evening Post*, 8 May 1951.
3   *Muddling Through Bristol in the Fifties*, Redcliffe Press, 1988. p26.
4   *Looking Back on Bristol, Hartcliffe People Remember*, Bristol Broadsides, 1978.
5   *Remembering Hartcliffe, the first twenty years*, Hartcliffe History and Education project, 1996.

Looking through the window of an Easiform flat as a policeman stands guard at the entrance on the day of its opening. Hareclive Road, Hartcliffe, Bristol. 30 November 1952.

Introduction

I moved to Hartcliffe in December 1964; I was 10 months old. For my parents getting their own council flat was a huge achievement; at the time they were living in a room in an auntie's house in Knowle West and before that in private rented accommodation in Southville. A council flat meant security. In 1988 I was elected as the Bristol city councillor for Whitchurch Park ward, which included most of the Hartcliffe estate, and remained the representative until 1999.

In the late 1990s I started to research the history of the estate. At that time, apart from a pamphlet by Bristol Broadsides, there were no publications which charted the history of Hartcliffe and the other post-war council estates of Bristol. There are many books exploring the history of the city which appear to think the city boundary stops at the edge of Bedminster. It felt that working-class communities did not deserve recognition. In his 450-page opus *Design Control in Bristol 1940-1990*,[6] the very time during which Hartcliffe was built and developed, John Punter mentions the area only once, in a throw-away line: "Residential development was to be encouraged on the periphery in large estates at Southmead, Lockleaze, Lawrence Weston and Hartcliffe." Almost as if there was no planning history to these estates worth mentioning, that a city is only its central area.

I quickly found (with the help of the staff of the Bristol Archives) the original plans for the estate and the committee papers which supported them. I was immediately struck by the amenities originally included in those plans and how the grand designs for the estate withered away over time, discarded and forgotten. This publication explores those original plans and how Hartcliffe was betrayed.

This story could be written about many post-war estates built on the edges of our towns and cities. It is as much a story of post-war Britain as it is of one estate. So why is it important to highlight Hartcliffe as a metaphor for the failure of post war austerity? Well, firstly, as I grew up and lived there, I am personally invested in Hartcliffe's history but, also, because so many battles were played out in the development of the area including:

---

6 Punter, John V., *Design Control in Bristol 1940-1990*, Redcliffe Press, 1990. This is a standard academic work on post-war planning and was presented as the comprehensive review of planning policy in Bristol (and elsewhere) for the decades following WWII into the modern era.

- ◆ Building of homes versus the retention of farmland;
- ◆ The resistance to expanding city boundaries;
- ◆ The tension between housing numbers and housing quality;
- ◆ Universal provision versus means testing;
- ◆ The inability to fund community facilities in a period of shortage and austerity;
- ◆ The emergence of comprehensive education and its challenge to the tertiary system;
- ◆ The challenge to involve local residents in community activity;
- ◆ The fight for co-education;
- ◆ How changes in the political control of the council impacted upon the area during its development.

While some of these conflicts can be found on other estates, it is doubtful that all of them are replicated in any other single location.

Later publications, which are referenced in this book, had a tendency to highlight the positive stories about the estate, probably in response to the stigma which is directed to council estates. However, although well intentioned they give an unbalanced view and fail to hold those in authority to account for the failures in the design of the area and the real difficulties which people there experienced.

1. Homes after the war

In January 1943, the fortunes of war were changing. The Soviet Union was winning battles in Leningrad and Stalingrad, islands were being recaptured from the Imperial Japanese Army, but the clearance of the Warsaw Ghetto was being accelerated and the bombing of British cities by the Luftwaffe continued.

Although the end of the war was to be over two years away, thoughts of post-war reconstruction had already begun in Bristol and the council's housing committee received and approved a 'Plan for Post War Housing', stating that the "preparation of the post-war programme must not be delayed if your Committee are to be ready to commence building to meet the housing needs of the people at the close of the war".[7]

This housing report was framed within a national context of renewal. While there was a recognition that there would be a shortage of materials, it was agreed that "the priority given to house building will have to be very high indeed, even if it is not the highest of all".[8] It was also agreed that "Your committee consider that adequate steps should be taken to ensure that houses built in the future are the highest standard compatible with the purpose for which they are intended".[9]

The report sets out the impact of a combination of the poor quality of some existing housing, damage caused by the war and demographic change. In particularly purple prose it states

> Bristol is built in one of the most beautiful parts of England, and it has great natural assets. If full advantage were taken of its hilly nature Bristol would indeed be a beautiful City, but although some of its buildings and streets give pleasure there is no gainsaying the fact that a great deal of man's handiwork has produced unnecessary ugliness and squalor. It is only necessary to visit parts of Barton Hill, St Philip's, St Paul's, St Augustine's, Bedminster, Easton and others and see the dilapidated conditions which exist, to understand that no longer should the broad scale of this problem be deferred.[10]

7 Bristol Council Housing Committee, Report, 12 January 1943, Bristol Archives.
8 Ibid.
9 Ibid.
10 Ibid.

Alderman Hennessy (left) and Alderman Gill (right) were driving forces in Bristol's post-war reconstruction.

It also quantifies the short-term need for 18,600 new homes:

Overcrowded Families	1,000
Couples married during the war	10,000
Families rendered homeless by enemy action	2,400
Families with children living in rooms	4,000
Families occupying houses required by owners for their own accommodation	500
Single aged persons	500
Aged married couples	200

Over the longer term the minimum number required was 30,000: the 18,000 above, 7,000 to replace homes unfit for human habitation and 5,000 for household growth.

Unfortunately, the council was only able to identify 4,000 available building plots, half of them in Southmead, far short of the land needed for 30,000 homes. The committee agreed to urge the government to:

> ...relax existing regulations both labour and materials as to enable Local Authorities to put in hand the complete repair of all houses damaged by enemy action which can be made habitable ... At the earliest possible moment to permit Local Authorities to resume the building of housing ... The preparation now of a plan for building homes adequate to meet the known needs of the nation ... Action by the Government to protect Local Authorities from exploitation by landowners, industrial and commercial interests.[11]

The report came back to the housing committee in September 1943. The council received genuine support from the Minister, however this was only for the plans and not for immediate house building. It was expected that the new programme would adopt the pre-war programme of around 2,000 homes each year, starting with sites identified in the earlier report, mainly Southmead, Horfield and Knowle. The council also agreed a programme of repairing war-damaged houses (it identified that 76,897 homes had been damaged by bombing) and requisitioning empty homes.

Extending the city

The council realised that it could not meet the need for new housing within the city boundary. At its meeting on 9th November 1946, the council received a report from the Planning and Reconstruction Committee. The investigations into extending the city's boundary were set to start on 28th November 1946. The report states, "The fundamental factor in considering the question of boundary extensions is the number of dwellings".[12] That number is calculated within the report:

> The estimated number of dwellings required ... is 60,692 and there are within the City, either in private ownership or in the ownership of the Corporation, sites for around 12,500

11 Ibid.
12 Planning and Reconstruction Committee report to the City Council, 9 November 1946. Bristol Archives.

dwellings, leaving 48,192 dwellings to be provided outside the present limits of the City, or say 50,000 in round figures. On the basis of 3.5 persons per house, this involves housing 175,000 persons which would require at least 17 neighbourhood units.[13]

It adds that,

It is not sufficient, however, to have regard to the number of dwellings in considering the question of the future size of the City. It is the determined policy of the City Council to plan the provision of housing accommodation not in aggregation of dwelling-houses but in neighbourhood units. Each of which should comprise a population of about 10,000 with the schools, clinics, churches, shops, open spaces, community centre, library etc, necessary to ensure that each unit is a community in the fullest sense of the word.[14]

The area within the urban fence provides a basis for the discussion of boundaries. As will be seen from the map it comprises Filton, Kingswood, Mangotsfield, with subsidiary areas outside the main area of urban development … the extension of the City should be such as will enable the required number of neighbourhood units to be provided, within the urban fence and subsidiary areas if it is possible to do so. The main urban fence area plus the subsidiary areas at Warmley, Long Ashton and Portishead would give room for fourteen out of seventeen neighbourhood units. The remaining three neighbourhood units could conveniently be placed on the lower slopes of Dundry Hill without serious infringement of the landscape.[15]

The discussions had commenced prior to this report. On 13th August 1946 the city clerk set out the position following a discussion with the Boundary Commission. His report stated "…discussions at officer level had been initiated with Somerset and that there were to be discussions with Gloucester early in September, also that it was possible the city council would be in a position to formulate proposals some time

13 Ibid.
14 Ibid.
15 Ibid.

in October".[16] The report again emphasised the importance of housing in driving the need for boundary extension:

> The question was really finding space for the overspill from Bristol. There is a waiting list of over 20,000 applicants and there was a population of about 50,000 which would be taken out of Bristol by reason of slum clearance, etc. To some extent the figures overlapped, but at any rate there was the problem of finding room for housing 50,000 people. If the housing was to be carried out by the City then the boundaries would need to be extended.

The Hartcliffe site was mentioned in this report:

> In the discussions with the officers of the Somerset County Council, the officers of the City Council had put forward the suggestion for the development of the lower slopes of Dundry Ridge on the south of Bristol, and Keynsham.[17]

The following day, the story appeared in the *Bristol Evening Post*:

> Extension of Bristol's city boundaries to what is known as the "urban fence" considered by many to be the most likely of alternatives now under consideration – would, I am told, mean an expansion to the limits of local urban development. Filton, Patchway, Kingswood and Hanham, Staple Hill and Mangotsfield all lie within such an area, but are not included in the present Bristol boundaries.[18]

The battle of Bristol's boundary had begun.

Opposition from the areas outside the city was huge and vocal. The *Bristol Evening Post* reported alternative plans by Kingswood, Mangotsfield and Warmley to merge to avoid "absorption into Bristol".[19] The *Western Daily Press* reported on a meeting of Portishead Urban Council declaring "Portishead wants freedom ... The urban council is to take every step possible to oppose the Corporation's plans to incorporate

16 Report of the City Clerk, 13 August 1946. Bristol Archives.
17 Ibid.
18 *Bristol Evening Post*, 14 August 1946.
19 *Bristol Evening Post*, 18 September 1946.

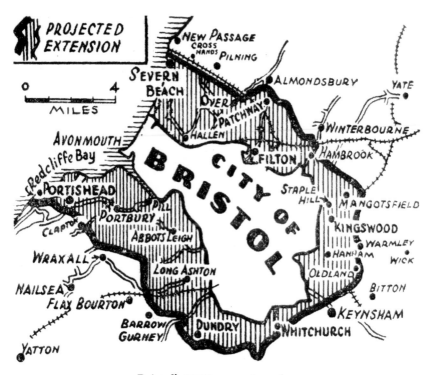

Bristol's 1946 expansion plan.

Portishead district within the city boundary". The Portishead council clerk said:

> My impression was that it was nothing more or less than a farce. We could see from the plan that it was proposed to include Portishead. Your delegates went there to find out the reasons why in their wisdom they propose to include Portishead with Bristol. I am afraid we came away almost as ignorant as when we attended.[20]

The *Bristol Evening Post* published a map of the proposed city extension on 5th November 1946.

A strongly worded letter to the *Western Daily Press* from F Taylor from Willsbridge started:

20 *Western Daily Press*, 5 November 1946.

There is no difference between Hitler's "Lebensraum" and Hennessy's "Living space". Out of the same vintage and same bottle. But we resisted Hitler's aggression. Cannot we do the same to Hennessy and his ilk?[21]

Alderman Hennessy, a leading council figure, replied:

It is because of these outrageous conditions under which our people are living that, Hitler or no Hitler, we must extend our boundaries well into the countryside.[22]

The commission came to Bristol in November while outrage continued to fill the columns of the local papers and their letters pages.

The future of farmland on the northern slopes of Dundry Hill was bound up in this debate as it lay outside of the city boundary but was being regularly referred to in Bristol's housing plans.

Neighbourhood units

The idea of the 'neighbourhood unit' was adopted by many cities after the war.[23] It was both effectively national government policy and also endorsed by the wider planning sector. One of its proponents was Paul Cadbury[24], from the famous Quaker Family which had built their own version of a neighbourhood unit (the Bournville estate in Birmingham) dating back to 1900. In promoting the idea through the New Towns Bill the Minister, Lewis Silkin MP, identified an even earlier antecedent, although the principles being applied were the same as for the city-based neighbourhood units:

My researches on new towns go back to the time of Sir Thomas More. He was the first person I have researched I have discovered to deplore the "suburban sprawl," and in his "Utopia" there are 54 new towns, each 23 miles apart. Each town is divided into four neighbourhoods, each neighbourhood being laid out with its local centre and community feed centre.[25]

21 *Western Daily Press*, 13 November 1946.
22 Ibid.
23 Boughton, John, *Municipal Dreams, the rise and fall of council housing*, Verso Books, 2018
24 *The Times*, 13 October 1945.
25 *Hansard*, 8 May 1946.

In his promotion of new towns, Silkin also warned against building new estates on the edges of existing towns:

> Many towns have built new housing estates on the outskirts. These have largely failed in their purpose of providing a better life for people and have almost invariably become dormitories consisting of members of one income group, with no community life or civic sense.[26]

The New Towns were modelled on Ebenezer Howard's idea of a 'garden city' so it is interesting to see that the Dundry Slopes estate is sometimes described in the local media, particularly the *Western Daily Press*, as a 'garden city'. However, this idea, which clearly influenced the neighbourhood unit concept, assumed that the new garden cities would be separated from the central city by countryside and linked by railways.[27]

In its influential 1943 publication, *Rebuilding Britain*, The Royal Institute of British Architects describes people wanting some amenities in easy walking distance, including small shops, a café, a pub and a nursery school. This would need a population of around 1,000 people which would form "the smallest unit of our City".[28] It then suggests we might need larger shopping areas for the weekly shop, a restaurant, places of worship, a library, a community building, a health centre, and schools. For this larger area it proposed:

> About five thousand people can support a junior and senior school that are educationally about the right size, neither too small not too big, so let us suggest that five of our residential units should make up a neighbourhood, and share these schools and other amenities, and that this neighbourhood should also be planned in such a way that it has coherence of its own. Such a neighbourhood would probably need offices too, and perhaps might have some small local industries, like bakers and cobblers and laundries. It should certainly have a park, with the buildings set in it in groups.

26 Ibid.
27 *Rebuilding Britain*, RIBA (Royal Institute of British Architects), 1943.
28 Ibid.

This vision was adopted by the national government. In the *Housing Manual 1944* it set out guidance for the building of new housing and communities. The first section of the first chapter was titled "The Neighbourhood":

Where big authorities must build a very large number of new houses, it may be possible to plan a new self-contained community based on a new centre of employment. In such a community due regard must be paid to industrial, social, educational, and recreational centres and their relations to the new development as well as to accommodation for the different classes of people who make up a well-balanced residential neighbourhood. The scheme must not be planned simply as a dormitory without a recognisable centre; it should include shopping facilities, schools, churches, and the other communal buildings frequented in everyday life, so as to meet practical needs and at the same time lead to a sense of neighbourliness among the families who go to live there ... every effort should be made to ensure that so far as possible the facilities are ready by the time the bulk of houses are occupied. The absence of such facilities at the outset inevitably causes discontent among the tenants and gives the new community a bad start. A population of roughly 5,000 to 10,000 affords a convenient basis for a neighbourhood.[29]

Bristol enthusiastically embraced the 'neighbourhood unit' concept, and the idea set out in the 1945 book *English City, the Story of Bristol*.[30] This was published by another chocolate manufacturer, J S Fry and Sons, but from its credits was clearly written by Bristol city council officers and distributed to Bristol's school children. The book set out the ambition in a section titled "Planning by Neighbourhoods":

In some parts of Bristol lack of planning in the past has resulted in the unhealthy crowding together of factories and houses, with no space for gardens, parks and playgrounds. On the other hand, the siting of housing on the outskirts has often meant that workpeople have had to spend an unnecessary amount of time and money in travel to and from their work.

29 *Housing Manual* 1944, Ministry of Health, Ministry of Works, 1944. p.11.
30 *English City, The Story of Bristol*, J S Fry and Sons Ltd, 1945.

One solution to the problem is to plan the city in self-contained districts called "Neighbourhood Units", each with its own amenities, including a shopping centre, clinic, schools and churches, cinema and recreation grounds. Factories should be built in or near the "Neighbourhood".[31]

These 'neighbourhood units' would almost exclusively be built away from the city centre (where, in the diagram, the roads lead to) and the council was committed to extensive 'slum clearance' in central areas such as St Philips. The Housing Strategy of 1943 stated:

Your Committee consider that full use should be made of any powers to exist or which may be available later for the purpose of clearing completely areas of the city by means of Compulsory Purchase Orders [CPOs] in an orderly and planned manner, so that the redevelopment, either for housing, industrial purposes or open spaces shall be in accordance with the major plan adopted for the City as a whole.[32]

In describing the 1944 Reconstruction Plan, John Punter notes:

The careful segregation of land uses into "precincts" mean that much of the mixture and diversity of central city land uses was doomed. Most importantly the plan spelt the end of the central city as a residential area. Although some seven specific locations were zoned for residential use these were small and presumably intended for public housing. The area south of St Mary Redcliffe was set aside for large scale redevelopment as flats for "key workers" (docks, railways and local industry) but otherwise residential development was to be encouraged on the periphery in large estates at Southmead, Lockleaze, Lawrence Weston and Hartcliffe.[33]

As quoted earlier, the council identified that three neighbourhood units would be on the Dundry Slopes. Those three neighbourhoods would become Hartcliffe (two of them) and Withywood (the third).

31 Ibid.
32 Bristol Council Housing Committee, Report, 12 January 1943, Bristol Archives.
33 Punter, John V., *Design Control in Bristol 1940-1990*, Redcliffe Press, 1990.

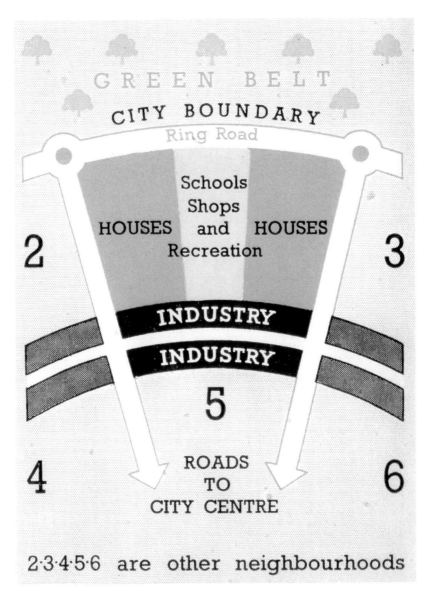

Bristol's neighbourhood unit model.

Hartcliffe from the air.

2. The battles for the Dundry Slopes

Bristol council started working on the plan for Dundry Slopes while it still lay outside of the city boundary. The issue of jurisdiction delayed the development as Bristol and Somerset debated the transfer of land and populations between them.

In July 1947, the *Bristol Evening Post* reported:

> Bristol City Council, with a long term building programme involving the provision of some 60,000 dwellings are seeking land on the northern slopes of Dundry on which to build houses for Bedminster workers.[34]

It explained that meetings were being held with both Somerset County council and Long Ashton district council. The article went on to say:

> In view of the substantial number of Bristolians who were employed in the Bedminster area, land had to be found in the south of the City … The areas suggested are mainly below the 300-foot contours and in no case above the 450-foot contour.

> In the event of the Boundary Commission not including the area now under consideration the county council is asked to agree to a review of county districts under which the area would be transferred to the city.[35]

While the proposed boundary changes to the north and the east of the city in Gloucestershire and the coastal areas including Portishead and Clevedon were controversial and attracted substantial and sustained opposition, changes to the sparsely populated area on the Dundry slopes appear to have been much less controversial.

In November 1947, the city council reported on a meeting with the chairman of the Boundary Commission, Sir Malcolm Trustram Eve (Lord Silsoe). The report stated that the meeting had been informal and should be treated as strictly private and confidential.[36]

At this stage the Boundary Commission was prepared for Kingswood, Warmley, Patchway, Filton, Winterbourne, Almondsbury

34 *Bristol Evening Post*, 16 July 1947.
35 Ibid.
36 Report to the Planning and Reconstruction Committee, 19 November 1947.

and Mangotsfield to come within the city, but for Portishead to stay outside and that Bristol's land around Portishead docks should be moved out of Bristol and into Somerset. The report also seemed to suggest that if Bristol achieved a population of greater than half a million people, it would have to become a county with two districts at the second tier.

Returning to the Dundry Slopes the report concluded:

> Bishopsworth, Whitchurch and the Dundry area—Sir Malcolm pointed out that the urban fence line in this area was shown as following approximately the 400ft contour of the Dundry Hills but that a new major road was planned so that it included Whitchurch and Bishopsworth on the inside but that the whole of the proposed neighbourhood units on the Dundry Hills were outside this road. Sir Malcolm was informed that discussions were taking place with the Ministry of Transport with a view to the line of this road being altered to run along the outside edge of the proposed new neighbourhood units. He indicated that, provided the line of the road could be agreed, the Commission would raise no objection to the land required for the three neighbourhood units being within the City. He also agreed that Bishopsworth should be inside the City but that the Commission did not agree at the moment that Whitchurch should form part of the City.[37]

Three points here: first the council was considering a major road running above the housing estate along the Dundry Hill, something which never made it into any formal plans, probably due to cost and logistics; second that the Boundary Commission was supportive of Dundry Slopes becoming part of the City; and thirdly, that Whitchurch village would retain its status outside the city, but that Bishopsworth would be incorporated into Bristol. The council agreed:

> ...to appoint representatives with the officers to meet members and officers of the Somerset County Council in order to discuss the development of the Dundry slopes; the proposals of the Boundary Commission with regard to Whitchurch, and the possible inclusion of Ashton Court Estate within the City.[38]

37 Ibid.
38 Ibid.

This view became a public position when the recommendations of the Local Government Boundary Commission were published in April 1948. Summarised in the *Bristol Evening Post*:

> The Greater Bristol of the future embracing Filton, Patchway, Kingswood U.D. [Urban District], Mangotsfield U.D., and parts of Whitchurch and Bishopsworth will have a population of 500,000 and will extend between 40,000 and 45,000 acres.[39]

The report made it clear that, if there was a dispute between councils, the process of changing the boundaries could take up to two years. However, this timescale could be significantly shorter if there was an agreement between councils. There was also a new map of the proposed boundaries.

The talks between Bristol and Somerset continued and, in May, the latest position came back to the council:

> A letter from the clerk of the County Council stating that, after discussions with the Long Ashton and Bathavon Rural District Councils, the County Council were unable to agree to cede to the City the areas comprising Whitchurch, Bishopsworth and Ashton Court, and were prepared to agree to a transfer to the city of the portions of Dundry Slopes required for housing purposes and included in the Compulsory Purchase Order already made. The County Council had also adhered to their view that the part of Portishead at present within the City boundary, the Ham Green area and the foreshore to a point near or beyond Clevedon pier should be returned to the administrative County of Somerset.[40]

Despite the approval in principle, to transfer the portions of Dundry Slopes referred to in the letter, arriving at a formal agreement was dragging on. So the city council decided to press Somerset County on the implications of a large housing development just within its northern boundary:

39 *Bristol Evening Post*, 8 April 1948.
40 Bristol City Council, 5 May 1948, Bristol Archives.

The Town Clerk reported that in the course of his negotiations with the Somerset County Council to obtain their consent under section 81 of the Housing Act 1935, he had pointed out to the Clerk to the County Council the obligations which would fall upon the County Council owing to the Dundry Slopes being outside the city boundary. Following upon this the Somerset County Council asked for an interview with the Boundary Commission and the chairman of this committee.[41]

Bristol piled on more pressure.

The City Engineer reminded the committee that during the discussions with the Boundary Commission it was made clear that the Commission attached considerable importance to the section of the Outer Ring Road to the south of the City being planned clear of all foreseeable City Housing Development, and as a result south of the proposed housing development on the Dundry Slopes … The S.C.C. were very anxious to ensure that it was accepted as falling within the amended City boundary as they feared it might be recast and planned to the south of the Dundry Ridge through County areas rather than to the North of the ridge.[42]

This pressure must have helped to move County Hall as a letter was sent to Bristol at the end of the month which contained this stunning paragraph:

The County Council now find themselves in a very difficult position in that they will have the responsibility of providing local government services for the occupants of the houses which Bristol are proposing to build on the Dundry Slopes. This undertaking will involve the County Council in vast expenditure in respect of an area of the County which the Boundary Commission have already indicated should be added to Bristol, and may have the effect of disorganising the whole basis of County Council administration.[43]

41 Bristol City Council, 1 December 1948.
42 Bristol City Council, 15 December 1948.
43 Letter from Somerset County Council, 31 December 1948, Bristol Archives.

Bristol's revised expansion plan 1948.

Somerset was becoming concerned that Bristol might push ahead with the building of the neighbourhoods but leave Somerset holding the baby of providing a wide range of services to the people who lived there. The Dundry Slopes development would have quickly become the size of a Somerset town on the far reaches of the county, an hour away from Taunton.

A report (set out in detail in Appendix 2) was presented, in a private sitting, to a joint meeting of Bristol's Housing and Planning and Reconstruction Committees which assessed the practical, financial, legal and even democratic challenges of having a significant population living just outside the city's boundary with services provided by a confusing mixture of Bristol city council, Somerset County council and Long Ashton district council. The report concluded: "it has been necessary to draw attention to the absurdities of the situation in which the City and the County Council are placed".

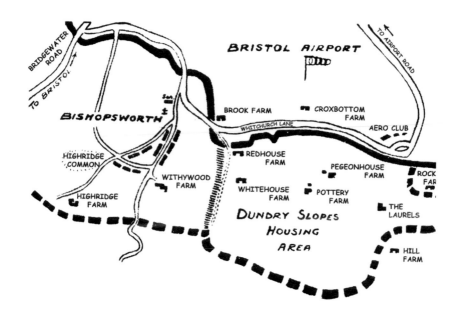

The farms of the Dundry Slopes.

Reading this report one can only imagine the sense of frustration that councillors and their officers must have been feeling. If they take the extension which has been agreed in principle on the Dundry Slopes they are likely to lose the opportunity to expand the boundaries into Gloucestershire. If they don't expand into Dundry, the house building policy collapses, or, if they build an estate outside of Bristol, there would be a confusing network of council responsibilities for the area. One doesn't even have to read between the lines to guess the exasperation of the report's author, summarised in the use of the word 'absurdities'. There is also a sense of desperation that wrangling over boundaries would sabotage the city council's plans to meet its large and growing housing need.

Also standing in the way of constructing the estate was the ownership of the land. Three farms occupied the area and to build the homes the council needed to purchase the land, by compulsion if necessary. The CPO was applied for in April 1948 and contested by the main farmers affected; the inquiry was held in January 1949.[44]

44 *Western Daily Press*, 8 and 12 January 1949.

Mary James, a great niece of Bill Withers, was one of those farmers; she recalls, "My mother and father were very upset, the farm had been in the family for a very long time, but when you tenant a farm, you don't build up capital very well, so you couldn't go and buy another farm".[45]

The report of the inquiry in the *Western Daily Press* was vivid with description:

> Over the centuries the lush green slopes of Dundry Hill have looked down on the sprawling growth of Bristol and all that time they have brought in turn a glimpse of the countryside to the heart of the city.
>
> Whether future generations will see this unique feature untouched by the rapid development of the city, was weighed in the balance at Bristol Council House yesterday.
>
> Bristol Corporation anxious to acquire the northern slopes of this famed beauty spot for a new township—neighbourhood unit—battled with the farming community whose land was wanted.
>
> The Corporation said they had no intention of building all the way up the slope, and gave assurance they would not spoil the skyline.[46]

The lawyer representing the farmers stated:

> In my submission it is abundantly clear that my clients are really the victims of an appalling lack of foresight by those who have charge of the housing policy of this city.
>
> I suggest that Dundry should have been the very last place where they ought to go to put a satellite town. It is a unique feature that is enjoyed consciously or unconsciously, and one would have thought strenuous efforts would have been made to maintain it.

---

45 *At Home on the Slopes, A history of Hartcliffe & Withywood*, Neil Beddow/ACTA Community Theatre Ltd, 2002. p.19.
46 *Western Daily Press*, 12 January 1949.

Even if the houses are not built all the way up, I suggest the rising smoke from houses will obscure the skyline.[47]

Inevitably the council was awarded the compulsory purchase and this barrier to building the estate was removed.

Mary James reflected, "I remember mother and father extremely worried about what they were to do, and that the landlord was looking for compensation. Well he got compulsory purchase money, but it was not worth very much so we had to put up with what we had and left".[48]

The decision was announced to the people of Bristol on 1st March 1949. Under the headline: "Bevan Decides—Dundry Slopes for Housing", the Western Daily Press reported:

Delay is inevitable and contractors will not move in on Dundry much before Christmas. Eventually the dormitory town will hold 10,000 people. Bristol Corporation made local history by seeking housing land outside the city boundaries, but Dundry will not be the last such project.[49]

The report made it clear why the housing pressure was immense: "A hundred new applications for Council houses are entered every week … 'Live' applications now number 15,631".[50]

The lobbying to extend the boundaries continued. In April, councillors travelled to London for a meeting with the Boundary Commission. However, in June the announcement came from the government that it was winding up the Commission. Now extensions could only be achieved by mutual consent.

In August, housing committee chairman, Charles Gill, was reported as telling the committee that he thought it was "very possible" that Somerset County council would agree to the extension of the Bristol Boundary to include the new Dundry housing estate.[51]

In September a report came to the council setting out the options for a deal.[52] The first option was to give up on a boundary change and to have "a continuation of the 'Dundry Slopes Expedient'".[53] This would

47 Western Daily Press, 12 January 1949.
48 At Home on the Slopes, A history of Hartcliffe & Withywood, Neil Beddow/ACTA Community Theatre Ltd, 2002 p.19.
49 Western Daily Press, 1 March 1949.
50 Ibid.
51 Western Daily Press, 3 August 1949.
52 Bristol Council, 13 September 1949, Bristol Archives.
53 Ibid.

leave the area outside the city and all the problems outlined in the January 1949 report. There was a remote hope that a future government might agree to an extension. The second was to continue to push for a boundary extension, but this would be limited to the areas which could be agreed with the county council.

The report explained the deal which had been hammered out with Somerset County:

(a) That the City Council will raise no objection to the following areas at present within the City being transferred to the County:-

(i) Such parts of Portishead and Ham Green as are within the City; and

(ii) Clevedon Pier Head and that part of the foreshore of the Severn westward from Portishead Point.

(b) That the County Council and the appropriate District Councils will raise no objections to the following areas being transferred to the City:

(i) an area of Stockwood which is the subject of a report which is being submitted to the Council by the Housing Committee at this meeting;

(ii) the village of Bishopsworth and an area of Bishopsworth, which is also the subject of a report to the Council by the Housing Committee at this meeting;

(iii) The Dundry Slopes (excluding Dundry Village) to an agreed boundary below the ridge;

and

(iv) Some 75 acres forming the lower portion of Ashton park, which is required by the Education Committee for school purposes.[54]

54 Ibid.

On 4th October Somerset County council approved this plan.[55] The ministerial order changing the boundary officially came into effect on 1st April 1951.

The government killed off any hope Bristol had to further extend its boundary to the North and East:

> There had been contacts with the Ministry of Health, who had indicated that the agreement between Bristol and Somerset had, in their opinion, very much reduced the urgency of any extension into Gloucestershire at the moment, and that owing to uncertainty as to the policy which was to follow the dissolution of the Local Government Boundary Commission the Minister was not inclined to approve anything but the minimum boundary extensions for the time being.

and

> In any case, the extension of Bristol into Gloucestershire would present far more difficulties than an extension into Somerset, since the City would have to absorb very considerable rateable value before reaching any land which could be suitable for large-scale housing development.[56]

The proposal was for the surrounding districts to build and manage the additional housing required by Bristol. In the following years Bristol built council housing for other councils (called overspill estates) but with no long-term interest in them, including homes in Kingswood, Warmley, Hanham, Yate, Keynsham and other areas which it had originally sought to absorb.

Bristol had originally sought to expand over an enormous part of the surrounding of around 37,000 acres. After three years of lobbying and negotiations, that had reduced to 1,600 acres, less than a twentieth of the original proposal. However, the Dundry Slopes was now under Bristol's control and a new housing estate, township, neighbourhoods or garden city (depending upon which newspaper articles you read) would be planned and built there.

---

55 *Western Daily Press*, 5 October 1949.
56 Ibid.

3. The grand plan

With the boundary and land ownership settled, Bristol could now bring forward the plan for the Dundry Slopes. Officially reported to councillors in January 1950, one can only assume that the plan had been gathering dust for some time in anticipation of the opportunity to build the neighbourhood within an expanded city boundary. The plan for the area exactly reflected the neighbourhood unit ideal.

The name for the community had not been settled and the report was snappily titled "A brief report of the proposed development of the Dundry Slopes Compulsory Purchase Order for the Housing Committee of the Corporation of Bristol".[57] The report was accompanied by a large-scale plan which illustrated the layout and amenities of the neighbourhood.

It must have been exciting for councillors on the committee finally to be able to take forward such a significant development, which had initially appeared as a proposal in council papers in 1946. A large development like this would also take a significant chunk out of the council's housing waiting list. It could also be an exemplar of the 'neighbourhood unit' model.

Below are extracts from that report:

Acreage

The gross area of this site is approximately 680 acres. Of this, for various reasons, some 140 acres are to revert to farmland, leaving a nett area of 540 acres for development as a neighbourhood unit.[58]

The land excluded from the development was farmland above the building level or which was too steep to develop, much of this would eventually form the Hartcliffe Community Park Farm, which was opened in the late 1980s.

---

57 Bristol Housing Committee, 24 January 1950, Bristol Archives.
58 Ibid.

The plan also describes the development as a 'neighbourhood'. In earlier documents it was described as three neighbourhoods on the Dundry Slopes, one of which would later be Withywood, so this area should have been two neighbourhoods; redesigning it as one would clearly reduce the need for two centres of shops and community facilities and hence the cost.

Future Roads

The whole of the vehicular access to the estate now and when completed will be from the East, North and West sides. No access can be made from the South partly due to the nature of the ground, but partly due to the proposed outer ring road, which skirts the southern boundary of the site to which no vehicular access from the estate will be permitted.[59]

The outer ring road is not shown on the map. There is a reference to the outer ring road in the 1930 Abercrombie plan for Bristol and Bath: "...it by-passes Bishopsworth village on the south, via Highridge Common; after utilising the existing lane between Bishopsworth and Whitchurch it affects another by-pass at Whitchurch and crosses the Wells Road".[60]

However, this road would run partly through the proposed estate. A road to the south of the estate doesn't seem feasible as it would be running fairly high, just below the ridge of the hill over very difficult terrain. Somerset were worried that the building of the homes could push the ring road to the south of Dundry Hill which would, one could imagine, generate enormous protest from the villagers in that area.

It is also interesting that the report discusses the ring road being to the south of the estate but that there would be no access to it, so the residents would gain the pollution and noise from a ring road but not the benefit of being able to use it. For these reasons, and probably more, it was never built and, at the time of writing (2023), the arguments over the route of the ring road were still a subject of great dispute.

It is pointed out that the main access to this development is by way of these roads, and should they not be provided at an

59 Ibid.
60 Abercrombie, Patrick and Brueton, Bernard, *Bristol and Bath Regional Planning Scheme*, 1930.

early stage of general development it would mean the housing provisions would not be served by public transport.[61]

As we will see later this did come to pass and was a bone of contention for the early residents (or pioneers as some described them).

Estate Roads

... It is now suggested that the latest recommendations of the Ministry of Health regarding minimum widths of highway and footpaths should be adopted throughout.

Briefly these are as follows:

Cul-de-sacs etc	13ft. carriageway	6ft. footpaths
	10ft. "	6ft. "
Minor Estate Roads	16ft "	" "
Bus routes	22ft "	" "

This minimum has, however, been broken in two cases, those of the two main bus routes. Here the roadway will be in both cases 30 feet.[62]

In many cases these road widths did not allow spaces for cars to park and the provision of garages on the estate was minimal. It appears that it was thought that working-class people would not generally own cars and would be dependent upon the bus service to travel to work or the city centre attractions of leisure and retail.[63]

Airport

In view of the existence of the Bristol Airport in the near vicinity, the Ministry of Civil Aviation has imposed height restrictions

61 Bristol Housing Committee, 24 January 1950, Bristol Archives.
62 Ibid.
63 Ravetz, Alison, *Council Housing and Culture: The History of a Social Experiment*, Routledge, 2001. p.103.

on the adjoining development ... This height restriction zoning has been the virtual sterilization of the eastern portion of the site as far as normal housing is concerned. This has meant, of course, the concentration of such activities as require no building above the 10 feet restriction height in this area, i.e. School Base Playing Fields, organised games and allotments.[64]

Bristol Airport was not relocated until 1957 so its location during the early phase of development dictated the geography of the estate, with the secondary school placed at the eastern edge of the land such that the main areas affected by the height restriction were the school playing fields.

A report in the *Western Daily Press* claimed the airport almost killed off the whole project. The headline—"Dundry Garden City Plan Has Been Saved"—is also a spoiler alert. It explained:

> A Civil Air Ministry muddle "wiped out" the Dundry garden city a month ago! This story was not told to Bristol Housing Committee when they approved the development plans yesterday, because a behind-the-scenes appeal saved the scheme.
>
> The project is held up now as the city waits for Whitehall permission to build roads to Dundry ... The last "attack"—from the Ministry of Civil Aviation—caused the biggest shock of all. Just after Christmas the Ministry issued a new set of flying restrictions affecting buildings which made it virtually impossible for building to be carried out on the slopes.
>
> Difficulties over the nearness of Whitchurch aerodrome were foreseen when the City Council first approached Somerset County Council for the transfer of the land, but under the compulsory purchase order these points were dealt with satisfactorily, or so everyone thought.
>
> Of the 540 acres some 58 were covered by height restrictions forbidding building of more than 10 feet in height and this area was allocated for playing fields and an open space.

---

64 Bristol Housing Committee, 24 January 1950, Bristol Archives.

Mr H. M. Webb, City Planning Officer, was quick to inform the Air Ministry of the prior agreement ... the new order was quashed within a week.

"Already we have been forced more on to the slopes by the aircraft—and that in itself adds to the cost of building," Mr Webb said yesterday. "And then, when the Ministry issued their latest regulations, it looked as if they wanted to re-model the whole site to suit themselves".[65]

The article goes on to describe further representations on extending the inner ring road to the estate and describes the facilities which will be built there.

<u>Existing Farms</u>

The farms which lie within the areas to be developed are:

1. Pigeon House Farm.
2. Pottery Farm.
3. Whitehouse Farm.

Of these Pigeon House Farm houses will be completely demolished, Pottery and Whitehouse Farm houses should be converted and used as Youth Clubs.[66]

Whitehouse Farm was on Hareclive Road opposite the junction with Murford Avenue, Pottery Farm was on Grinfield Avenue and backing onto Faber Grove, and Pigeon House Farm was on Briscoes Avenue.

The engineer in charge of installing the drainage system, a Mr Hubbard, had the distinction of being the first resident of Hartcliffe. He moved into the now abandoned Pottery Farm, which later survived for some years as a Methodist church, probation office, meeting place for the scouts, before falling into ruin and eventually being demolished.[67]

65 *Western Daily Press*, 24 January 1950.
66 Bristol Housing Committee, 24 January 1950, Bristol Archives.
67 *At Home on the Slopes*, ACTA Community Theatre, 2002. p.23.

Proposed Layout

The development shows the site traversed by two main roads ...
The higher of the main roads is taken out on the west side of the
development where it will continue across the Bishopsworth
development, forming a bus route and the main traffic link
between the two housing units.[68]

The higher road referred to here is Bishport Avenue. The 'Bishopsworth
development' was renamed Withywood following objections to its
original name.[69]

The housing has been grouped about these two main through
routes with the object of keeping access on to these main roads
to a minimum.[70]

The major streams crossing the site are preserved for the
following reasons:

(i) That the volume of discharged water and the rock subsoil
would make it uneconomic to culvert them.

(ii) That the streams can be used for storm or surface water
disposal.[71]

Housing

The general housing provisions are envisaged in two, three and
four storeys, and it is suggested that terraces be employed to a
great extent wherever practical.

The exact type of accommodation is of course, a matter for
further discussion, but it is estimated that some 3,100 dwellings
can be accommodated within the area.[72]

---

68 Bristol Housing Committee, 24 January 1950, Bristol Archives.
69 Harris, H.C.W., *Housing Nomenclature in Bristol*, City and County Housing Department, 1969.
70 Bristol Housing Committee, 24 January 1950, Bristol Archives.
71 Ibid.
72 Ibid.

Schools

Four school sites are suggested, 3 junior and infant schools of 8.75 acres each and a senior school base of about 60 acres. In addition 6 nursery school sites of 0.75 acres each are suggested.[73]

The three schools became Whitehouse and Hareclive, facing each other across Hareclive Road, and Teyfant which was located to the southeast of the estate sharing the land reserved for the secondary school for Hartcliffe.

Youth

Three youth club sites are suggested one being Whitehouse Farm and one Pottery Farm. Both these are existing buildings which may be converted for use as a Youth Club. The third will be a new building erected in conjunction with the senior school base.

In addition to these, a site for a scout hut and a separate site for a guide hut is reserved on the southern boundary where direct access be had to the countryside.[74]

These scout and guide huts were to be at the end of Bouchier Gardens and at the top of Aldwick Avenue. "A youth section will also be incorporated in this main community centre adjacent to the shopping centre".[75]

Community Centre

A site for the Community Centre is reserved in the central shopping area immediately adjoining the swimming bath and cinema site. It has a wide frontage and sufficient depth to accommodate court games and gardens. It is suggested that these should have joint use with the swimming bath.[76]

73 Ibid.
74 Ibid.
75 Ibid.
76 Ibid.

From the map the extent of the gardens planned was substantial, effectively covering almost all the area occupied by the three Silcox Road multi-storey flats, presumably to allow for tennis and other courts.

Clinic

A Health Centre site is suggested on the north side of the central road near the main shopping centre. An effort has been made to keep this site as near the first stage housing as possible without isolating it from the main centre.[77]

Not mentioned in the report were also a small number of doctors' houses and a dentist's house built on the estate. These were larger than the council houses as the doctor lived mainly upstairs with their consulting room downstairs.

Library

A library site has been suggested on the south side of the main shopping centre.[78]

For many years the estate was served by a mobile library service.

Swimming Bath

The site of the proposed swimming bath is immediately adjoining the Community Centre and garden.[79]

Cinema

A site for a cinema is provided in the main centre adjoining the shops and main bus routes.[80]

77 Ibid.
78 Ibid.
79 Ibid.
80 Ibid.

Shops

These have been arranged in one main group in the Civic Centre, with three subsidiary groups suitably placed within the development. The main centre could accommodate approximately 20 shops units, and the subsidiary centres approximately 6 shops units in each. A certain flexibility is being retained in siting the shops pending the results of investigations which are now being carried out.[81]

Churches

Three church sites have been suggested, two on the axis of the main shopping centre and one at the junction of the Bishopsworth and Dundry development to the west.[82]

This provision does not include a site for a Catholic church. The two churches on the axis of the main shopping centre were the Anglican St Andrew's in Peterson Square and the Methodist on Moxham Drive. A Catholic church was later built on the east of Hareclive Road and the Christian Fellowship was built near the junction of Teyfant Road and Bishport Avenue. The Pentecostal church was located near the junction of Hareclive Road and Murford Avenue. There was no provision for any other religions.

Aged Persons Homes

Two sites for aged persons homes are suggested adjacent to the main shopping centre. On each of these a hostel for 40 persons will be erected.[83]

Public Houses

Sites for six public houses have been suggested within the development, two of these will be adjacent to the main centre,

---

81 Ibid.
82 Ibid.
83 Ibid.

and the remaining four suitably placed within the development, and in the vicinity of the subsidiary shopping centres.[84]

The pubs plus the small clusters of local shops were to be built to form the 'residential units' mentioned in the RIBA publications referred to earlier, seeking to create distinct local communities within the overall development with the pubs acting as local community hubs.

Service Industry

It is suggested that any service industries such as laundries, bakeries, etc. should be located in the light industrial area proposed on the north side of the link road.

Housing Maintenance Depot and Transport and Cleansing Accommodation

It is suggested that the main Housing Maintenance Depot be located in the area between Dundry and Bishopsworth development. This site being central for the two areas. A secondary Maintenance Depot is suggested within the Dundry development to the east.[85]

The housing office was also located here. It is interesting that in all the talk about neighbourhood units there was never a proposition that they should have any democratic autonomy or buildings such as a town or village hall. The Community Centre was never proposed to be akin to a town or parish hall, with no idea of locally elected representatives undertaking 'parish' type activities. The council did not propose a 'civic' building in the main centre and the housing office was hidden away on a site well away from the retail centre. The council would control the area (one of the issues underlying the boundary review) but none of that control would be ceded to local residents or institutions.

84 Ibid.
85 Ibid.

Public Lavatories

Sites for four suggested public lavatories will be suitably allocated throughout the development, one of which of course, will be adjacent to the main centre.[86]

Organised Games

An area of the east of the site is suggested for organised games. It is suggested that a changing pavilion, café and paddling pool should be erected to serve this area.[87]

This area is also the location of the secondary school, on land where the height restriction enforced by the airport meant that housing could not be built.

Land Reverting to Farming

It is suggested that a considerable portion of land on the east and three portions of land on the south of the site should revert to farm land. These areas are either too steep to develop or are of an unsuitable shape and it is felt that they cannot be economically developed.[88]

Much of this land would eventually become the holding of the Hartcliffe Community Park Farm and totalled over 100 acres.

Spare sites

Certain areas of land within the development have not been allocated for any specific purpose at this juncture and it is felt that they should be left in order to accommodate any future requirements which are not specifically known at the moment.[89]

There is an appendix to the report summarising the use of the 540 acres, in detail and in summary.

86 Ibid.
87 Ibid.
88 Ibid.
89 Ibid.

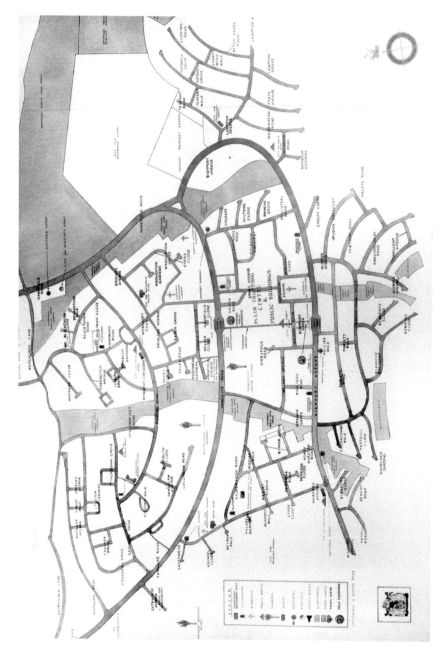

Revised plan for the Dundry Slopes produced by the housing department, July 1958.

SUMMARY

Schools	90.75 acres
Public Buildings	26.50
Open Space	108.75
Housing	<u>314.00</u>
	540.00

Total estimated number of dwellings—3,100 units.

Gross density: approximately 5.80 [dwellings] per acre at 3.8 persons [per] tenancy—22.00 persons per acre.

Nett density approximately 10 [dwellings] per acre.[90]

Calculating that another way, with 3.8 people per property and 3,100 properties the estimated population was 11,780.

This was an ambitious plan which followed the 'neighbourhood unit' model almost to the letter (although it was technically two neighbourhood units with the central facilities for one). A genuine new community with a wide range of facilities to accompany the houses was envisaged.

The plans clearly grabbed the imagination of one journalist, his excitement and enthusiasm could hardly be contained within the page. This was seen as truly a wonderous dream of an amazing new community being built of the slopes:

> As much work has gone into Dundry as in the planning of satellite towns in other parts of the country and when finally the garden city arises it will be a venture of which Bristol will be justly proud, and it will have been built without marring the famous skyline view of the Slopes.[91]

Naming and shaming

Looking north with views of the city is the village of Dundry, a mining area at least as far back as Roman times. Dundry church was built by the Society of Merchant Venturers, partly to act as a beacon to Bristol

90 Ibid.
91 *Western Daily Press*, 24 January 1950.

sailors who could see it from far out at sea to confirm that they were nearly home.[92] Dundry also gave its name to the Hill which sets a natural southern boundary to the city, rising over 700 ft and stretching for two miles.

The proposal of a new Bristol Corporation estate reaching half-way up the hill was not welcomed by the villagers. The idea that it might also have Dundry in its name was seemingly abhorrent.

In June 1950, the housing committee heard:

> The Town Clerk reported that a letter had been received from the Clerk of the Parish Council of Dundry enquiring whether it was the intention to use the name Dundry in connection with the above Estate, in which case it was desired to register a protest and draw attention to the confusion and complication likely to arise.[93]

The minutes go onto describe a less than sympathetic response:

> After discussion, during which it was suggested that the name should be New Dundry, or the existing village re-named Old Dundry, it was—RESOLVED—That the Town Clerk be asked to discuss the suggestion with the Parish Council and the Postal Authorities.[94]

The response came back very quickly and was reported to the next meeting only two weeks later:

> Arising out of the Minutes, the Town Clerk reported that he had conveyed to the Clerk to the Dundry Parish Council the suggestion that the new estate at Dundry Slopes should be named 'New Dundry' and had received a reply to the effect that they objected to the name 'New Dundry' and had conveyed that objection to the Postal Authorities. After discussion it was RESOLVED—That the Town Clerk and the Housing Manager be requested to give consideration to the selection of a name for the estate.[95]

92 Mee, Arthur, *Somerset*, The King's England, 1949. p.168.
93 Bristol Housing Committee minutes, 5 June 1950, Bristol Archives.
94 Ibid.
95 Bristol Housing Committee minutes, 19 June 1950, Bristol Archives.

Housing manager Mr Herbert Harris, the man who named Hartcliffe.

Still moving amazingly quickly for a local authority, a proposal was brought to the committee at the following meeting. The city council had conceded to the parish council and the proposed name had no reference to Dundry:

> It was suggested that 'Hartcliffe' might be appropriate in view of the fact that the area, so far as could be ascertained, was largely in the Hundred of this name ... Resolved That the name of Hartcliffe to be approved.[96]

Interestingly the new name was suggested by Mr HCW Harris,[97] who later went on to write *Housing Nomenclature in Bristol*, the definitive guide to the meanings of council housing street and flat names in the city.

But what does it mean?

96 Bristol Housing Committee minutes, 4 September 1950, Bristol Archives.
97 *Western Daily Press*, 5 September 1950.

In *Housing Nomenclature*, the full definition can be found not under 'Hartcliffe', which just references the Hundred, but within the section naming of one of the main streets on the estate, Hareclive Road:

Hareclive was the original form of Hartcliffe. According to Collinson, Hare is derived from a Saxon word signifying army, whilst Clive is a steep rugged rock or cliff. Many battles are believed to have been fought in this area in the days of the Ancient Britons.[98]

Given more recent history the name may well have been prophetic, Hartcliffe is the army on the hill.

This didn't settle the legitimacy of the name. Was Hartcliffe really in the Hundred of Hartcliffe? Harris clears this up in the introduction of *Housing Nomenclature*:

When the Housing Committee finally agreed to the name of Hartcliffe, press publicity was given to certain objections to the name on the grounds that the estate was not in the Hundred of Hartcliffe, but of Dundry. The decision of the Committee was eventually justified when a reporter of the old *Bristol Observer* [now defunct] made a thorough investigation and proved beyond doubt that much of the site was in the Hundred of Hartcliffe.[99]

The naming of the estate was not the last dispute over naming. Next came the street names. They had been agreed in July 1951; however, an attempt to change them was made in 1952. A councillor proposed:

In view of the country's wide remembrance of the Battle of Britain, I suggest that the streets on the new Housing site on Dundry Slopes should perpetuate the names of some of those airmen who took part. Can this be arranged, or alternatively, will the suggestion receive the consideration it deserves?[100]

The proposal was voted down as the city had a long-established policy of naming council housing streets and buildings based upon

98 Harris, H.C.W., *Housing Nomenclature in Bristol*, City and County Housing Department, 1969.
99 Ibid
100 Bristol Council minutes, 2 April 1952, Bristol Archives.

names with a historical connection with the area concerned. Again, *Housing Nomenclature* explains the background to the street names:

> The selection of names presented some difficult as there was little historical or any other background, but some use was made of Dwelly's National Records—Directory of Somerset, 17th Century Hartcliffe cum Bedminster Hundred (privately printed 1929) and various County histories and parish records and the Dundry Enclosure Award of 1815.[101]

101 Harris, H.C.W., *Housing Nomenclature in Bristol*, City and County Housing Department, 1969.

'Bishport Fives' under construction, 1964.

4. Building on the cheap

Everything was now set, the boundary had moved, the land was purchased and the plans approved. What could possibly go wrong?

There was no substantial road into the development area and Whitchurch Lane, which crossed the north of the site, was not sufficient to service the area. The aim was to bring the inner ring road to the estate and join it with the two planned main roads within the scheme.

In March the Planning and Reconstruction committee was advised that the government was not prepared to fund the expected £75,000 for the conveniently priced £99,000 project and that their contribution would be limited to just 50% of the cost.[102] The committee agreed to go back to the government seeking the higher level of support. The lobbying was unsuccessful, and the following was resolved at the council meeting held two months later:

> That in the circumstances the council be recommended to accept the Ministry's offer of a Class III classification and 50% grant towards the cost of constructing the length of road from Parson Street to Crox Top, but to inform the Ministry that such acceptance has been decided upon only because the Council will not accept the responsibility for the delays in the provision of houses on the Dundry Slopes which would otherwise ensue.[103]

This also meant that the new road would be a single rather than a dual carriageway. The contract to build the road was awarded to building company A E Farr Ltd for £93,695.[104] In May 1954 this contract figure was increased to £106,727, mainly due to rises in the costs of materials and labour.[105] A E Farr would later gain the contracts to build the roads, pavements and sewers across the estate.

In many respects this was the shape of things to come for the new development, as the funding became more restricted and the vision for the estate gradually evaporated.

---

102 *Western Daily Press*, 15 March 1950.
103 Council minutes, 3 May 1950, Bristol Archives.
104 Council minutes, 6 February 1952, Bristol Archives.
105 Council minutes 25 May 1954, Bristol Archives.

Housing Committee in session, 1957.

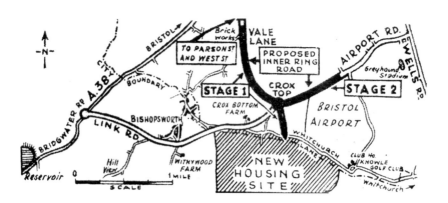

The Inner Ring Road was scaled back in 1950.

Politics

The timing of Hartcliffe coming together was also impacted by changes in the political environment. The decision to approve the neighbourhood was taken at the beginning of the 1950 general election campaign when the post-war Labour government saw its overall majority shrink from the landslide of 146 seats to a sliver of just five. At the time, the council itself was represented equally by Labour and Citizen Party[106] councillors and aldermen.[107] In 1950 the casting vote was held by Labour through the Lord Mayor whereas in 1949 it had been held by the Citizen Party.[108]

As the building in Hartcliffe started, the Citizen Party won control of the council for the first time since the end of the war. They captured the council by taking Hengrove ward from Labour, which reflected their gaining the majority of the popular vote in the seats contested (the Citizens also won five unopposed seats by default).[109] The swing to the Conservatives was further confirmed in the snap general election held in October that year.

In June the Citizens pursued a policy, later adopted by the Conservative government nationally, of cutting the standards for new council housing.

Housing Standards

In 1945 the council had committed itself to building high quality homes. The *Bristol Evening Post* reported the chairman of the housing committee, Alderman Gill, as saying that despite difficulties with gaining access to materials, the new homes would be built to a high standard. The *Post's* headline was "Standards must be higher, New Homes for Men who return from the forces"—not quite homes for heroes but the intention was clear.[110] The Minister for Health and Housing, Nye Bevan, had ambitious plans to build council housing after the war. He declared, "While we shall be judged for a year or two by the number of houses we build ... we shall be judged in ten years' time by the type of houses we

---

106 At the time, in Bristol, the Conservatives and (some) Liberals stood together under the Citizen Party banner.
107 Aldermen were a type of representatives without a ward, allocated to reflect the seats won in the annual elections.
108 *Western Daily Press*, 12 May 1950.
109 *Bristol Evening Post*, 11 May 1951.
110 *Bristol Evening Post*.31 October 1945.

build".[111] He also wanted council housing to be suitable for people from all walks of life:

> It is entirely undesirable that on modern housing estates only one type of citizen shall live. If we are to enable citizens to lead a full life, if they are each to be aware of the problems of their neighbours, then they should all be drawn from different sections of the community. We should try to introduce what was always a lovely feature of English and Welsh villages, where the doctor, the grocer, the butcher and the farm labourer all lived in the same street.[112]

To reinforce the universality of council housing under the Labour government resources were restricted such that 80% of all homes built were council housing.[113]

The report to the new Citizen-majority housing committee in June foreshadowed the approach of the Conservative government elected a few months later. The headline in the *Bristol Post* was very different "Building of Cheaper Council House: Plan is Accepted." The article goes on to report the discussion: replacing sliding doors with swing doors between rooms would save £4 on the cost of a house; perhaps dividing walls could be removed altogether and replaced with curtains; reducing ceiling heights could shave another £10 to £20 off the price of a house. The Committee were told that the price of a new house could be brought down to £1,120.[114] The Citizen Party only held power in Bristol for one year. However, the lower housing standards were retained by Labour, once they were re-elected in May 1952 as the national picture had changed. The archives don't show the issue of council housing standards being raised after Labour's return. The only reference in the media was in a newspaper comment from the Citizen's Party when seeking re-election in 1953: "On housing, our policy is to build more houses at a cost better related to what the average tenant can afford. During our year in office, we introduced economies in house building. The Socialists opposed these economies but are now quite happy to continue them".[115]

111 Boughton, John, *Municipal Dreams: The Rise and Fall of Council Housing*, Verso, 2018.
112 Ibid.
113 Ibid.
114 *Bristol Evening Post*, 4 June 1951.
115 *Bristol Evening Post*, 5 May 1953.

The autumn Conservative government was committed to seeing 300,000 council homes built per year. Harold MacMillan, the housing minister and later Prime Minister, was successful in reaching this target but,

> Another factor in Macmillan's quantitative success was a sharp reduction in council housing quality. The so-called People's Houses, which formed the bedrock of the new programme, were marked by reduced space standards. New ministry guidelines announced in 1951 made Bevan's 900 square foot minimum for a three-bed house a maximum; henceforth new council houses were again—at between 750 to 850 square feet— significantly smaller.[116]

Under the Conservative government there was also a shift in emphasis from houses to flats and in the mid-fifties the subsidy system was changed to favour high-rise development, leading to 11 high-rise blocks being built in Hartcliffe and Withywood in the late 1950s and early 1960s.[117]

This emphasis on building as many houses as possible meant providing services and communal facilities would take a back seat.

Much is made of Hartcliffe's lack of social diversity; however, it was designed under a Labour government which saw council housing as providing homes for a range of classes, as illustrated by the Bevan quote. It was then built under a Conservative government which saw council housing as being homes for the poor or at best a steppingstone to home ownership where people would only stay until they could afford to buy a home.[118] With a renewed emphasis on home ownership under the Conservatives, council housing estates became less diverse. The social mix of the Hartcliffe which was built did not match the vision of when it was planned.

Another area of diversity is that of race. The Empire Windrush docked in London in June 1948, as people from Britain's colonies responded to a call for labour to rebuild the country and to work in the expanding health service. As a port, Bristol had a long history of immigration as well as its well-known involvement in the shameful slave trade. Local authorities with already long waiting lists often excluded

---

116 Boughton, John, *Municipal Dreams: The Rise and Fall of Council Housing*, Verso, 2018.
117 Ibid.
118 Ibid.

the newcomers from council housing, some introducing an onerous residency requirement of up to three years.[119] In Bristol too there was a waiting time to get on the list of six months, a residency requirement (which isn't specified in the records) and additional points based upon how long you were on the list. The weighting based upon time on the list became more significant in each annual update of the system during the 1950s.[120] The waiting list was very much a time-ordered list, people would need to demonstrate they were of good character (for example only married couples were permitted to apply for houses). Representations to a local councillor or member of parliament carried weight in the system. I met people who would name local politicians who had 'got them their house'. This was reflected in the demographics of Hartcliffe. When I was a child on the estate, I was aware of only two non-white families—being one Indian and one Chinese (out of almost 4,000 households). Bristol was not unusual in this:

> People were normally precluded from applying to a waiting list if they did not live or work in the district, or had not done so for a specified period of time … It was this requirement, above all, that excluded recent immigrants, who were affected by other exclusions as well. For instance, they often initially lived as single men and women, or cohabited rather than married, while if their families were with them these were often too large for any houses available. Together with the fact that they were frequently ignorant of the rules and their own entitlements, this explains the great under-representation of ethnic minorities amongst council tenants through the 1950s and 1960s.[121]

Building the homes

Council minutes (too many to reference individually) located in the Bristol City Archives, in some cases detail the actual cost of the homes and the types built. Most were constructed using non-traditional methods of building, often grouped together as Pre-Reinforced Concrete (PRC) homes. In 1984 legislation was passed forcing councils to repair

119 BME national website, *Our Roots*, https://bmenational.co.uk
120 The Housing Report, Bristol Corporation 1955, 1956, 1957 and 1958. Bristol Central Library B14100.
121 Ravetz, Alison, *Council Housing and Culture: The History of a Social Experiment*, Routledge 2001. p.130.

Homes in Hartcliffe.

Cornish Unit cul-de-sac.

homes which had been sold under the Right to Buy scheme, as such systems were later found to be defective. Water penetrated the homes, rusting and expanding the steel structure which in turn started to crack the concrete panels, accelerating the deterioration.

28th May 1952[122]	48 E (economy) type houses, Traditional Build.
	Gatcombe Road, Horesham Grove, Coleshill Drive and Lyvenden Gardens.
	These were three-bedroom houses, total cost £71,029. Average cost £1,529.
9th Sept 1952	162 Cornish Units.
	20 one-bed flats, 128 three-bed houses, 14 four-bed houses.
	Build cost £223,723, departmental charge £4,566. Average cost £1,409. Builder: Selleck Nicholls & Co Ltd.
9th Sept 1952	172 Laing Easiform Houses.
	75 two-bed, 92 three-bed and 5 four-bed. £249,796, department charge of £4,976 Average cost £1,481. Builder: John Laing & Son Ltd.
9th Sept 1952	108 Laing Easiform Flats.
	108 two-bed flats in nine three storey blocks. Cost £153,920, department charge £3,764. Average Cost £1,546. Builder: John Laing & Son Ltd. [I suspect these are the flats on Gatcombe Road/ areclive Road.]

---

122 Dates relate to the committee date of the report. The level of detail varies by what was published in the minutes.

16th Oct 1952	180 Cornish Units.

60 one-bed flats, 16 two-bed flats, 36 two-bed houses, 16 three-bed houses, 52 four-bed houses. Total Cost £259,590 plus £6,040 departmental charges. Average cost £1,446. Building contractor: Selleck Nicholls & Co Ltd.

Cul-de-sacs off Blackthorn Road, Murford Ave and Wymbush Crescent.

29th Apr 1953	50 Unity Houses and 48 Cornish Units

Briscoes Ave, Wroughton Drive, Wroughton Gardens and Dyers Close

19th May 1953	300 Easiform Homes.

Contract price £438,409. This contract was changed 4 months later: "At the equest of the Ministry of Housing and Local Government, the contract has been varied by substitution of 24 three-storey two-bedroom flats for 16 two-storey two-bedroom flats (making 308 dwellings in total) at an increased price of £13,710 10 shillings … which includes an estimated sum of £300 for abnormals". This council minute shows the level of involvement of national government in local decision making and also the government's push to increase numbers by building medium-rise flats rather than two-storey buildings; an example of quantity trumping quality. The average cost of £1,468. Builder: John Laing & Son Ltd.

9th Feb 1954	56 Unity Houses.

Contract price £83,818, departmental Charge of £2,548. Average cost £1,542. Builder: Western Homes and Estates Ltd.

25th May 1954	112 Unity Houses.

Contract price £163, 921, departmental charge £6,500. Average cost £1,522.

25th May 1954	180 Cornish Units.

Contract price £259,590, departmental charge £3,150. Average cost £1,460.

25th May 1954	48 Traditional Houses.

Contract price £71,029, departmental charge. £1,100. Average cost £1,503.

17th Oct 1956	194 Reema Homes.

72 one-bedroom flats, 16 two-bedroom flats, 90 three-bedroom houses and 16 four-bedroom houses. Contract price £298,310 and departmental Charge £6.050, Average cost £1,569. Builder: Stone & Co (Bristol) Ltd.

17th Dec 1956	110 Cornish Homes

36 one-bedroom flats and 74 three-bedroom houses. Contract price £185,208 and departmental charge of £4,715. Average cost £1,727. Builder: Selleck Nicholls & Co Ltd.

14th Oct 1958   369 Traditional Homes.

141 two-bed houses, 212 three-bed houses
and 16 four-bed houses. Contract price
£391,612 plus department charges £28,559.
average cost £1,139. Builder: Holtby &
Dudman Ltd.

[This is likely to be in the Teyfant area,
an estate within Hartcliffe in the south
east, which had its own character and
identity, seen by some as the 'posh' end of
Hartcliffe.]

In 1961, an alternative approach was taken with a site for 53 homes prepared at Bishport Close and Kencot Walk, "On completion of foundation of each house the freehold of the plot will be conveyed to the purchaser of the house, total sale price of land being £14,575". The contract was issued to Wells (Builders) Ltd.

An office for the housing service was commissioned in 1955 and, then again, in 1956 when the original contractor withdrew. At that point it was called the "Maintenance Office and Resident Agents Office" and was built by John Knox (Bristol) Ltd for £19,927. The office was extended in 1960 for £1,519. This office was not in a prominent location or in the shopping area but was tucked away in a back land site behind between housing on the east of the estate, hidden as if an embarrassment.

These extracts cover over 2,000 homes with a total cost of just over £2.9m or £1,441 per property. The council contract records show that the eight tower blocks, commissioned in 1961 from Wimpey, cost just over £1.6m, around £3,000 per flat (£200,000 per block).[123] Excluding the high rises, the houses and flats in the area cost just over £4m. Trying to apply inflation to this figure to look at the build cost is difficult but between 1952 and 2022 inflation has increased prices by roughly a multiple of 36, which would mean the £1,441 of building a house then equates to around £52,000 now. Even being generous this is between half and a third of the cost of building a house these days. While the contracts allowed for economies of scale it is hard to conclude anything other

123 Bristol Housing Contracts, Bristol Archives.

Gardens behind the flats.

than these homes were built very cheaply, more so when one considers that the space standards were higher then than now. It is also worth noting that the PRC homes were not cheaper than the higher quality traditional built homes: their advantage was that they were quicker to build and could be built with a lower skilled workforce.[124]

Mud, mud, mud

You can't talk to an early resident of Hartcliffe, even today, without them mentioning the mud. As we already know, the estate is built on the side of a hill. Along the hill there are many springs, some permanent and others which only emerge following heavy rain. The topsoil is clay, which holds the moisture and also sticks to itself, reducing the drainage.

Here are some examples of residents' comments from existing published memories:

> We had a nice piece of mud. No streetlamps, no gateposts. There were two holes where the gateposts were going to be. You had to make sure when you came home at night, if you didn't have a torch, that you got dead centre, otherwise you went down the hole. Whichever way you went out of our road, after

124 Boughton, John, *Municipal Dreams: The Rise and Fall of Council Housing*, Verso, 2018. p.89.

it rained, you had a large puddle and you had to wade through it. *Sheila Horton.*[125]

The very first Hartcliffe residents waded their way through the mud to their houses in Coleshill Drive in the last week of October 1952 ... For the next three years families moved in their hundreds into Hartcliffe, and the one topic of conversation everywhere was 'Mud, Mud, horrible Mud'!! *Mr. Steadman.*[126]

I moved to Hartcliffe thirty-nine years ago, in 1957. Only part of the estate was built then. I can remember lots of mud because the roads had not been properly surfaced. *Pamela Winchester.*[127]

My first memory of the area is that it was muddy everywhere because the buildings and estate were still being developed. *Dianne Parsons.*[128]

My first impression was MUD. All you could see was loads and loads of MUD. To call it a road was a joke really the gardens were not sectioned off let alone the roads. You had no way of knowing where one road started and another began, only by asking builders or other women. We would walk over fields, muddy ground to get through to Bishopsworth for our doctors, shopping, anything required really. *Vera Harris.*[129]

In the beginning there was mud everywhere, brown sticky clay like mud! *Pat Peters.*[130]

We had no roads, no footpaths, no pavements. All we had was one road through the estate and a tiny bit of concrete in front of the door. Then a sea of mud. *Tony Driscoll.*[131]

125 *Looking Back on Bristol, Hartcliffe People Remember,* Bristol Broadsides, 1978.
126 *Remembering Hartcliffe, The First Twenty Years,* Hartcliffe History and Education Project, 1996.
127 Ibid.
128 Ibid.
129 Ibid.
130 *At Home on the Slopes, A History of Hartcliffe & Withywood,* Neil Beddow/ACTA Community Theatre Ltd, 2002.
131 Ibid.

Inside the Housing Office.

Housing Office & Maintenance Depot.

My eldest son was nearly four and I shall never forget it. He got out the van, and he had his best shoes on, and he went straight down through a mud hole. I'll never forget it, because there was no roads look, and no proper paths or anything. *Doris Bezzant.*[132]

It was a quagmire up here and across the road. Laings had a saw mill, and a workman's hut, so the lorries were constantly up and down the mud track. It was just mud, filthy mud. *Amy Pruitt.*[133]

The mud wasn't just the thing of memories. It was also extensively reported on at the time. The *Bristol Evening Post* even had a cartoon highlighting the Hartcliffe mud, published in November 1953, only a year after the first residents had moved in.[134]

The geology of the site was an issue long before residents moved in. The designers of the estate had to plan for the streams so gaps in the buildings reflected the temporary as well as the permanent streams. The approach to these streams also made things worse. To save money most of them were buried rather than culverted, which meant that the water running through them often found its way back to the surface when the weather was wet. My own memory is of one of these streams running through my garden, usually underwater, feeding a willow tree there and that pavements in Symes Avenue would often be dug up looking for a water leak when in fact a small spring had been reactivated.

Originally the two main streams running through the estate were to be features of the landscape. However, this would require road bridges which have a cost but, within weeks of agreeing the Hartcliffe masterplan, the housing committee had started cutting costs:

Because it will cost £25,000 more than a culvert, Bristol Housing Committee decided today by five votes to four not to build a bridge over a small river valley on the new Dundry Housing Estate ... It is necessary to carry three roads over various streams on the estate, and today it was agreed that in two instances block culverts should be built to sustain them. But in the case of the third—one of the main bus routes of the

132 Ibid.
133 Ibid.
134 *Bristol Evening Post*, 10 November 1953.

BEFORE ———— & ———— AFTER

HARTCLIFFE ESTATE

MUD

Once students of beauty were doting
On Helen of Troy, we agree,
And recently people were voting
For Garbo, or Vivien Leigh.

But mud-packs the girls have been using
Have worked such great wonders of late
That soon all the world will be choosing
THE BEAUTIES OF HART-CLIFFE ESTATE !

Evening Post cartoon highlighting Hartcliffe's famous mud, November 1953.

estate—the City Architect had recommended building a bridge to preserve the view which can be seen through the valley. The committee agreed in principle to this, but disagreement arose when it was found the bridge would cost £34,000. The Chairman (Ald. Chas. R. Gill) said a culvert would block out the view looking right down the valley. The additional £25,000 would work out at approximately £8 a house. Coun. K. A. L. Brown said the bridge was not really an amenity to the estate, and felt the saving of £25,000 could be much better spent—perhaps on a first-class meeting hall. The City Engineer

... said the proposed bridge was the cheapest possible one for the purpose, and it was not subject to Ministry grant because the road was not a classified one. Coun. A. L. Duggan said he would not vote for the bridge as it simply could not be afforded. Ald. Hennessy said the committee was taking a very short view. They should do everything possible to beautify the estate for the people who were to live there. "We should not be penny wise and pound foolish by adopting this policy of niggardly economy." Coun. Brown suggested it might be possible to erect the culvert at present and then build the bridge later, if the financial position improved.[135]

The stream to the east of the estate passed under Hareclive Road in a culvert. A bridge was never built. The stream which ran through the middle of the estate was just buried, saving the cost of two further bridges over Hareclive Road and Bishport Avenue. This policy of burying the streams has worsened the issues of mud and flooding across the estate to this day, ignoring the original plan's suggestion that the streams "can be used for storm or surface water disposal".[136]

As well as covering over the streams, the builders also ripped out almost all the trees and hedgerows; coincidentally it was only those on the banks of the one remaining stream which were protected. This issue was highlighted by local social worker, Deirdre Stanley, in an article published in the *Bristol Forum* magazine in 1960:

The impression given is almost of a military camp, something artificially made, pretty quickly, in an emergency, planned with deadly accuracy, hygienic and efficient for the most part, but lacking homeliness, or simply atmosphere. There is nothing with which a man might identify himself, no relic of the past, no hint of the rural country around, no connection with the city he has left behind. The vast few roads are so impersonal that they might be runways in a new aerodrome ... No cosy alley ways and country lanes, no corner shops and tiny roads here! No trees or bushes for hide-and-seek or courting couples: only grass verges ... so that to talk of preserving trees and farms and lanes and of encouraging offices and light industry to preserve

135 *Bristol Evening Post*, 27 March 1950.
136 Bristol Housing Committee, 24 January 1950.

atmosphere when one knew that these would only take up valuable housing space, would seem the height of fussiness and pedantry.[137]

However, all was not lost, Hartcliffe was not destined to become a concrete wasteland, Deirdre continues:

Much thought is going into this very problem of making the estate less of an estate and more of a place. Over 300 trees of all kinds have been planted in the estate over the last weeks and a Tree Wardens' scheme may do much to help them have a chance to grow.[138]

Someone driving into the estate today will be struck by the large number and height of the trees, particularly entering the area along Hawkfield Road. These giants are the result of the planting in the early 1960s, huge trees which were little more than saplings protected by wire cages and held up by wooden stakes when I was a young boy playing in the area.

Returning to the mud, one of the strangest stories, headlined "'Wonder' Cure Hartcliffe Soil Hopes", was reported by the local media in 1953:

An American soil-conditioner, which is said to "do wonders" to difficult soils, may help solve Bristol Corporation's problem to make earth fertile on the Hartcliffe Estate. The City Architect and the Housing Manager hope shortly to visit Long Ashton Research Station to discuss the use of soil-conditioner. For nearly a year Long Ashton scientists have been studying the process. The conditioner binds soil into porous lumps, enabling it to hold water without packing or becoming a gluey mud. The Agricultural Research Council of Great Britain are expected to make an announcement on the soil-conditioner soon when details of the research at Long Ashton will be given.[139]

No announcement ever came and there is no evidence that the soil in Hartcliffe was conditioned by the Corporation.

137 Stanley, Deirdre, 'An estate not yet a place', *Bristol Forum Magazine*, May 1960.
138 Ibid
139 *Bristol Evening Post*, 14 January 1953.

Open space.

The mud was not just to be a problem for the residents, but it also caused difficulties for workers on the site. In January 1952, headlined "Houses in ooze sea", the *Western Daily Press* reported on delays caused by the mud:

Water from hillside springs above Dundry, which has already drowned the hopes of an early home for many families on Bristol Corporation's housing list, claimed another victim yesterday. Work on electricity cables for the Corporation's proposed housing estate at Hartcliffe was interrupted while workmen helped to free a motor van buried axle-deep in mud on one of the estate approach roads. Following heavy rains last year, the springs in the area have been active. They turned the site at Hartcliffe into a sea of mud. Work on the preparation of sewers and drains has been in the face of great difficulties—and the pumps have been working overtime. One of the employees on the site said yesterday: "In some of the trenches—which are 15 feet deep—it has been like working in Niagara Falls. The water came at us faster than the pumps could take it away." One result of this has been that work could not be started on 442 houses scheduled for last year. The next instalment of 630 houses is still hanging fire and there is great danger of delay to other contracts. This may mean that Bristol's housing output will fall unless measures taken on other sites are successful. The water is also hampering employees of the South Western Electricity Board, who are laying cables on the site. One of the men working on the Whitchurch-Bishopsworth road said: "There has been a continuous stream of water coming down on us. It's been like that since we started laying cables in October".[140]

The following year there was a more dangerous incident:

> Two men working 11 feet down in a narrow drainage trench on the new Hartcliffe housing estate ... were trapped when the sides of the trench suddenly caved in. One man, Statton Szcoc (42) ... was hemmed in by the wet earth so that only his head showed, and it took his mates more than half an hour to dig him out. He was unconscious. He was taken to the B.R.I. by the City Ambulance with concussion and internal injuries and detained. His workmate, Thomas Douglas (31) ... was trapped waist-deep and managed to get himself out. He was also suffering from severe shock but was able to go home after treatment. "We were working about 20 yards from each other," Mr Douglas told the Evening Post, "The shoring and galvanised sheets suddenly gave way. The sheeting kept some of the weight of the earth off me, but Statton really caught it. I suppose the wet weather made the trench cave in".[141]

It didn't take long for the mud to become an issue for residents. After putting up with the mud for a year, residents from Coleshill Drive submitted Hartcliffe's first petition. Unfortunately, the petition itself has not survived (maybe it fell into a muddy puddle) however there is a minute of a visiting committee which captures its essence:

> The Housing Manager submitted a petition from tenants of homes in the vicinity of Coleshill Drive complaining about the condition of the roads and footpaths on the estate and refusing to pay any increase in rent until roads and footpaths were put into proper condition. The City Engineer informed

140 *Western Daily Press*, 24 January 1952.
141 *Bristol Evening Post*, 16 September 1953.

the sub-committee that arrangements had recently been made for temporary gravel footpaths to be laid soon after each group of houses was completed, but footpaths or the roads could not be fully made up until there was sufficient work to ensure continuity for the contractors.[142]

There is no record of what happened as a result of the petition or if the threat to withhold rents was followed. The implication of the minute is that the needs of the contractors trumped the needs of the residents and that little if anything was likely to change until there was a critical mass of paving work.

A few months later the *Bristol Evening Post* ran a feature about the estate, the headline once again highlighting the main concern of residents: "Mud a 'Bad Dream' One Day".[143] The article introduces the area as it was in 1954:

> The face of the lower Dundry slopes is rapidly changing as Hartcliffe, the Corporation's new housing estate, develops. In another two years 12,000 people will be living in what is described by Mr. J. B. Abbey, housing manager, as "the last of Bristol's semi-rural type housing estates".

The feature goes on to describe the facilities to be built which have been explored earlier here. Following the development catch-up, we come onto the state of the area, which highlights the mud mentioned in the title of the article:

> Tenants have to put up with the unavoidable mess of building equipment and mud which appears to be everywhere. Ask any tenant what they don't like about the estate, and the invariable reply is: "THE MUD."

Local residents gave their views to the reporter:

> As she wheeled a pram towards Hareclive Road (one of the estate's main roads), I met Mrs. Mavis Cox, of 27 Fulford Road, with her seven-month-old baby, Tony. Fulford Road is from the

142 Housing (viewing) Sub-Committee minutes, 12 October 1953, Bristol Archives.
143 *Bristol Evening Post*, 12 January 1954.

point of view of mud a road of parts. Says Mrs. Cox: "I have lived on the estate for three months and, like many of the other women, stay in rather than face the mud. I don't like the cold, but at least it makes going out a lot easier and cleaner." She hastened to add that where her home is the road is not too bad, and "Of course, we know these conditions won't last for ever." In Fulford Walk, where the roadway is only in the "foundation phase" mud is heaped up on the kerbside. A path has been laid, and tenants are content for the time being. They know that six months ago conditions were much worse.

At 19, Greenditch Avenue, I met Mrs. L. White and her two sons, Philip (5) and Barry (4) who moved into their new home from a flat in Frenchay on Monday. "How do you get out of here without getting caked in mud?" I asked. She replied, "Well so far, I've been more concerned in how to keep the mud out of here." Her back garden is at the moment a "no-man's land" with no footpath and the prospect of being really muddy when she ventures out as soon as the frost binding the clay together goes. She, like Mr. K. W. Cheeseley, over the road at no. 22 doesn't think the mud an insurmountable difficulty. But Mr. Cheeseley does think the road should have been named "Mud-ditch Avenue!" A tenant of eight months, Mrs Jean Weeks, of 85 Gatcombe Road comments: "About here, we'll be in clover as soon as the footpath is completed and the shops over the road open. I know what it's like for some of the newcomers, but like us along here, they'll soon find that at least most of the mud is just a bad dream".[144]

In the summer the *Bristol Evening Post* declared success in a further feature about the estate: "The mud is now a thing of the past and there is a row of five shops to meet immediate wants".[145] These were the first shops built on the estate in Fulford Road.

However, a couple of years later the weather overcame the area and the mud returned (if it ever left). In July 1956, and again in August, dramatic thunderstorms drove muddy water into the homes of residents.[146]

144 Ibid
145 *Bristol Evening Post*, 25 June 1954.
146 *Bristol Evening Post*, 19 July and 27 August 1956.

5. Building the community

Community Facilities

The punchline of this book could be that the majority of community facilities which were promised were never built, and many of those that were, followed much later than planned. The classic example of this is the Hartcliffe library, planned (some would say promised) in the original plan in 1950, but not opened until March 1974.[147] There is an interesting aside in the *Bristol Evening Post* in 1954, given the time taken to provide the facility:

> The Ministry of Housing and Local Government has lifted its ban on local authorities building libraries on housing estates and the Bristol Corporation is to make good the leeway lost under the ban.[148]

The report goes on to explain that the priority is to build one at Hillfields and then "next on the library list in Bristol come the Southmead and Filwood Broadway estates with other estates being provided with libraries 'as fast as possible under ruling economic conditions'".[149] 'As fast as possible' turned out to be 20 years.

The swimming pool never materialised and although a small pool was included in the Hartcliffe School East Building in the 1960s, it wasn't equipped as or run as a public facility. In nearby Knowle West, an estate built mainly in the 1930s, the council only got around to building their pool in 1962. Doomsday-Book-referenced Bishopsworth had a pool built in 1974 amid local campaigning in the area. Hartcliffe never fought for its pool.

The last reference to one being planned for the estate was as early as 1954. In a *Bristol Post* feature highlighting the poor provision across the City titled "The City of Swimmers … But Only FOUR Baths are modern", it explained:

> Bristol has fourteen swimming baths but only four of them, Bristol South, Jubilee, Speedwell and Shirehampton are regarded as very modern in design and construction … Since

147 *Bristol Evening Post*, 16 March 1974 and 19 March 1974.
148 *Bristol Evening Post*, 10 Dec 1954.
149 Ibid.

the war no city has been permitted to build a new bath. Money has been allowed for alterations and for bringing existing buildings up to date, but capital expenditure on work is not allowed. If it was, the Baths Committee would like to build a new pool at Filwood Broadway. This is where it is felt the need is greatest in the city and a site has been allocated for the building which it is estimated would cost £125,000. Application has been made to the Ministry for permission to prepare plans but so far it has been refused.[150]

This is yet another example of how dependent the city council was on approval from Westminster to rebuild Bristol. Under a subheading "Other Sites", the article goes on to say:

Apart from the Filwood Broadway site, Bristol has eleven others reserved under the Development Plan: they are at Southmead, Brooklea (St.Anne's), Beechwood Road, Manor Farm, Lawrence Weston, Hartcliffe, Brockhurst Road (St George), Stockwood, Henbury, Lockleaze and Bishopsworth. This is not the order in which they would be erected. No priority has been decided other than that the Filwood scheme should come first.[151]

With that, the pool in Hartcliffe sank beneath the waves, never to be resuscitated.

No sports pavilion with a public café was built either, the hillside scouting and brownie huts never rose and neither did the cinema. Again, Knowle West had a cinema built just before the war, now, like the swimming pool, demolished to make way for housing after many years of dereliction. Hartcliffe's cinema never had an opening night.

The land reserved for the pool, cinema and outdoor sports facilities attached to the community centre made way for three tower blocks. They also took the sports land and gardens which were promised to the Community Centre.

150 *Bristol Evening Post*, 26 Feb 1954.
151 Ibid.

The Community Association

A community association was successfully established on the estate as early as 1953. It held its first function in January 1954. However, at that point there was no community building in Hartcliffe so the event, described as "a concert-part social",[152] was held in St Peter's Hall, Bishopsworth. At that time, the *Bristol Post* was reporting:

> In case Hartcliffe Residents are wondering where their community centre is to be situated. I understand that Pottery Farm and the land immediately surrounding it has been reserved for such a building. The erection of a centre is still very much in the future. However, all association activities will be planned to increase the building fund. No chances will be lost in the hope that a community centre for Hartcliffe is not a too far distant prospect.[153]

Further progress was reported in April:

> Great progress has been made by Hartcliffe Community Association since its inception at the beginning of the year. A large membership has been built up and an extensive social programme and money has poured into the association's building fund. Earlier this week members approved the association's constitution, the appointment of officers and made suggestions for the future. Discussion was keen and lively. The principal outcome was that members have accepted a challenge from their committee on a money raising bid. They have undertaken to raise £750 by the end of September this year for the association's building fund. By that time plans for a community centre for the district will have been drawn up. If there is sufficient money in the building fund—and all members are determined that there will be—these plans will be submitted to the authorities for approval. Hartcliffe is certain that building work on the centre can progress before the association celebrates its first birthday.[154]

---

152 *Bristol Evening Post*, 25 Jan 1954.
153 *Bristol Evening Post*, 22 Jan 1954.
154 *Bristol Evening Post*, 18 April 1954.

An article specifically covering the development of the estate, published in June that year, was ominously headlined "Hartcliffe, The Battle to End Boredom Is Going Well...":

Like Rome, Hartcliffe cannot be built in a day. Until it is, a community association is doing valiant work helping to relieve some of the inevitable boredom that comes, particularly to the women who are at home all day, in beginning a life that is so vastly different from the one they have known in a crowded (perhaps overcrowded) street in the centre of the city.[155]

In the summer the association organised a carnival, with more money raised for the building fund, and the hopes for building a centre were still running high:

Mr K R A Bolan (chairman) reports, "Enthusiasm in Hartcliffe for community association projects increases week by week. If the authorities allow, and provided we can have suitable plans drawn up, we should be in a position to start on building a community centre towards the end of the year".[156]

The association was also prepared to enter the political sphere. In July, it hosted a public meeting with the local councillors following concerns about rising rents:

Irate tenants affected by the increased rents on the Hartcliffe estate bombarded two city councillors with questions at a meeting in Whitehouse school arranged by Hartcliffe Community Association ... On several occasions Mr Bolan had to appeal to questioners, all shouting at once, to give the speakers a chance to reply. More displeasure was expressed when it was announced that Housing Committee representatives would not be able to attend. More than 100 people were at the meeting.[157]

As the estate grew, it was decided to bring the professionals and the locals together into one body:

155 *Bristol Evening Post*, 25 June 1954.
156 *Bristol Evening Post*, 4 June 1954.
157 *Bristol Evening Post*, 31 July 1954.

So widespread is this development that many Hartcliffe people want an estate committee rather on the lines of the Lockleaze Joint Council. Preliminary meetings have been held to discuss setting up such a committee or council. A tentative suggestion for its title is the Hartcliffe Consultative Council. Members of the community association have conferred with representatives of Whitehouse Youth Club and each group committee will consider the matter aided by a draft constitution similar to that of the community councils of either Lockleaze or Southmead. Schoolteachers, clergymen, doctors, nurses and social workers will all be represented. Mr Kenneth Bolan, chairman of the community association, is strongly in favour of the proposal.[158]

In his book, *All Things New*, a guidebook on how to run a Church of England parish on a new estate, Derek Palmer, who was the vicar in Hartcliffe from 1959-63, reflected on the community association's relationship with the advisory council:

The professional Advisory Committee had done useful work in its early days but was wondering what its future was to be. The relationship between the two was hardly friendly and only a few people tried to bridge the gap.[159]

While the fundraising continued, not all events were successful. The community association experienced a financial loss of £15 on a concert that October. This poor performance was blamed on a council ban on smoking in the school hall where the event was held. This was the first issue that the community association wanted to raise with the embryonic group:

...the association will bring the complaint before the meeting on November 2 of those interested in forming a consultative council on the estate. They include representatives of organisations such as Whitehouse Youth Club and, it is hoped, local clergymen, doctors, nurses and the public. Mr J Dix, secretary of the association says "Can people reasonably be expected to shiver outside the school during winter concerts

158 *Bristol Evening Post*, 24 September 1954.
159 Palmer, Derek, *All Things New*, Star Books 1963.

and dances in order to get a smoke? They just won't come that's all".[160]

A follow-up report, a month later, seems to show that the smoking ban wasn't the root cause:

Despite the lifting of the no-smoking rule for such occasions only 42 attended the last dance, so Mr J Dix, secretary of the C.A. says that in future film shows for children and other entertainment may be arranged in the classrooms.[161]

One year into the community association's life, the building of the new community centre did not seem any closer:

Subject No. 1 on the agenda at the Hartcliffe C.A.'s annual meeting on January 25 ... will be the new community centre. Last week the executive committee was told it would cost about £3,000. A provisional site has been selected at the junction of Hareclive Road and Silcox Road [this is the site in the 1950 plan], but the association will have to find an initial deposit of £350 in the first year and a further £400 in the second before a substantial grant can be forthcoming. Each dance held by the C.A. loses money, but each week the deficit is diminishing. It is hoped to get a regular three-piece band to make the dance more attractive.[162]

A new reason was found for poor attendance at events:

At Hartcliffe, T.V. is being blamed for what Mr Dix, secretary of the association calls a "certain lack of community spirit." But here the association, only a year old next month, is breaking much new ground and ideas are a little slow catching on. Hartcliffe residents can show their community spirit on January 25. Much is to be discussed.[163]

160 *Bristol Evening Post*, 22 October 1954.
161 *Bristol Evening Post*, 26 November 1954.
162 *Bristol Evening Post*, 10 December 1954.
163 *Bristol Evening Post*, 31 December 1954.

Later, in 1960, a further suggestion for low involvement was provided by Tony Crofts writing in the *Bristol Forum* magazine in 1960:

Isolation. The word crops up again and again. Most of the men on the estate have an hour's travelling to get to work; many work as far afield as the B.A.C. or Avonmouth docks. They arrive home late in the evening, dirty and tired, and have to rest, wash, and eat a cooked meal before there is any question of going out. How much easier to doze off in front of the telly by a warm fireside. All the social leaders speak of the widespread apathy which faces any organised social endeavour. This is common to any area, particularly an exclusively working-class one, but it is understandable.[164]

The *Post* returned to this theme with an article updating plans for the estate:

Generosity and the community spirit will both be fully tested at Hartcliffe this year. Funds for three important buildings will have been opened before long. The first, which launched last May, is to provide money towards the £27,000 Methodist Church on the corner of Mowcroft Road ... Two other funds, to which residents will be asked to subscribe, are for the C.A.'s proposed centre in Hareclive Road and the Whitehouse Youth Club's multi-purpose centre at the junction of Hareclive, Fulford and Hawkesfield Roads. Hartcliffe C.A. will erect a board near the site for the new centre showing the progress of the building fund.[165]

Hartcliffe Advisory Council

The long-trailed AGM of the community association. was finally held and duly reported by the *Post*. However, in their report this is overshadowed by the creation of the Hartcliffe Advisory Council.

The launching of the Hartcliffe Advisory Council, under the chairmanship of Dr. Michard Lennard, has been the most

---

164 Crofts, Tony, *Bristol Forum 2*, May 1960, the Bristol Forum Trust, Ken Stradling Collection.
165 *Bristol Evening Post*, 21 January 1955.

important event for the estate. The council draws an impressive representation from all levels of life—doctors, clergymen, schoolmasters, representatives from the local community association and other organisations on the estate.

The theme of the annual meeting was the lack of support for practically all activities. Dance attendances were poor, and no one turned up for the clothing exchange scheme run by the Women's Committee with the W.V.S. [Women's Voluntary Services]. To combat the revenue drop caused by the lack of collectors, it was agreed to accept quarterly subscriptions of 2s. 6d. from each member instead of 6d. weekly. Mr. J. Dix (Secretary) considered this would provide a firm income of £500 a year, most of which would go towards the building fund. The association's first year resulted in a credit balance of £100. Maximum membership reached was 1,037. Mrs. A. Macpherson (secretary of the women's section) said the old-time dancing was in danger of closing down for want of support. Bearded Ken Bolan, retiring chairman, who is leaving the estate, was elected the association's first president in tribute to his work.[166]

This appears to be a dispiriting first year for the association. In *All Things New*, although disguised in the generality, Derek Palmer is clearly recanting the history of the Hartcliffe Community Association:

...there will probably be one thing in the new area, and it may be called different names, but in essence it is a 'Community Association' and such I shall call it. The pattern of these all over the country is remarkably similar. In the very early days of a new estate when there are few amenities or places of entertainment and everything is strange, there is a tremendous outburst of community spirit fostered among the mud! Newcomers are welcomed by old residents who have been there a whole month and know the ropes, and out of this there springs the desire to get together for two main purposes: entertainment, and the working for better conditions in the area. If a local school has been built, this becomes the centre for the Community

---

166 *Bristol Evening Post*, 28 January 1955.

Association, as it is probably the only public building of any sort. Here large socials and Christmas parties are held. Most areas decide to erect their own hall and start out with an ambitious building programme, often with voluntary labour. Hundreds of families join the Association and contribute quite large sums for the building. All this sounds fine, but after a couple of years the pioneering spirit begins to flag. The twenty volunteer builders begin to dwindle down to ten and then down to two or three, and often work grinds to a standstill. On the social side personal rifts start to destroy the friendly feeling and there is little trust. Those who were most willing to take the limelight in the early days often do not stand the pace, and because there is no accepted leadership individuals start feuds and resignations begin. All this while the ordinary member who has been paying for his centre has been sitting back, waiting for it to arrive, and when it doesn't complaints come pouring in.[167]

In March we get the first mention of the area's councillors playing an advisory local role:

Hartcliffe residents may soon be able to walk from classroom to classroom in Whitehouse school shedding their worries and problems as they go! Hartcliffe Advisory Council hopes eventually to install in the school an information and guidance bureau touching as many human problems as possible. Although this cannot be accomplished at once, a start is being made on April 19. Local councillors will be at the school between 7-9 pm, waiting to hear any resident's likes and dislikes about Hartcliffe. This will continue on the second Tuesday of each month. In addition to this, the Advisory Council is trying to organise in adjoining classrooms on the same night to give advice on welfare and perhaps marriage guidance.[168]

And there was good news for the community association too: "After its introduction the W.V.S. clothing exchange scheme, held in Lang's canteen, is now a tremendous success".[169]

167 Palmer, Derek, *All Things New*, Star Books, 1963.
168 *Bristol Evening Post*, 18 March 1955.
169 Ibid.

As summer events were prepared, the date for building Hartcliffe's Community Centre was, as reflected in Rev. Palmer's book, reported to be slipping further into the future:

This emphasises the need for that community centre! Officials, however, learn it will be two years at least before this materialises. So far, they have only two voluntary builders—an electrician and a bricklayer—registered and many more are needed on a list that has to be submitted to back the association's claim to the authorities for a grant to finance the work.[170]

The Advisory Council decided to highlight the issues facing the community:

A conference to be held at Hartcliffe on November 19 is believed to be the first of its kind to take place in the country. It will discuss "The problem of living in a new housing estate." Housing estate planners and the people who actually live in the "finished product" will discuss the advantages and drawbacks of living and working in such an area. Sir George Pepler, past-president of the Town Planning Institute, will give a general talk from the angle of those who plan the estate. The after-tea session will include a series of short addresses by people from Hartcliffe. Although speakers have still to be chosen, they will probably include a doctor, shopkeeper, social worker, schoolteacher, housewife and mother. Each will look at Hartcliffe from his or her own particular standpoint. Sir Philip Morris, Vice Chancellor of Bristol University will be in the chair and discussions will follow each session.[171]

The event was fiery. Headed "Hartcliffe planners come under fire", the *Bristol Evening Post* reported on a difficult meeting for those in authority. The report gives a good flavour of the debate and discussion and the disconnect between those who made the plans and the reality of living in them:

170 *Bristol Evening Post*, 24 June 1955.
171 *Bristol Evening Post*, 16 September 1955.

The Lord Mayor, Ald. Harry Crook, opening the conference said: "The day has gone by when a local authority can just put up houses for the people to live in and leave it at that." Sir George agreed with him. Houses should look and be homely he thought, but an estate needed more than that. "I think ultimately you want some spiritual and visual climax to the estate, just as we have in our old towns and villages", he declared. He pointed out that Hartcliffe would eventually be the same size as a town like Dorchester.

As soon as Sir George has finished, the questions came. He had spoken of estate planning on a national basis. His questioners focused their attention on Bristol, and mainly on Hartcliffe … What of roads? First came Mr R. Drissell. Could they not be laid out while the houses were being built so that "people can walk into their homes without having to strip off and change into other clothes", he wondered. Ald. C. R. Gill, chairman, Bristol Housing Committee replying said his committee was anxious to get people houses, so blocks of dwellings were given to various contractors. It had been impossible to get a "continuous run of road" from anyone.

Mr. P. Bezzant took the roads problem a little further. Sir George had said schools should be off main roads, and children should approach them along green walks. Mr Bezzant declared: "Obviously something has gone wrong with this estate. Right outside Whitehouse School there is a main road, with not even a footpath to walk on." Seven children have been killed in accidents on the estate. Did Sir George think grass verges gave children a false sense of security?" Sir George: "That is a very interesting point. The idea of grass verges was that they should act as a sort of buffer." Roads were too small on Hartcliffe, said a woman. There was hardly room for two lorries to pass. There was no park on which the children could play, so they used the roads instead, thought Mr. Abrams. Knowle West had waited 20 years for one. "Make certain you get a public park," he urged.

Ald W. H. Hennessey, chairman of the Planning Committee, had the last word. Many complaints would be remedied, he said, "but give us a chance." Hartcliffe would not be perfect but they had tried to plan it as near-perfect as possible. "When you contrast Hartcliffe with Knowle West. You see there has been a complete revolution in the planning of housing estates in this generation".[172]

It is unclear what if anything changed as a result of this event. It did highlight a disconnect between the theoretical view of estates and the practical experience of people who lived on them.

The claim that seven children had been killed on the estate's roads is a shocking one. Such deaths are not always reported in the media. I can find no reference, for example, to a childhood friend who was killed by a lorry when crossing Hareclive Road in 1974.

One case that was reported gives a possible source of the 'seven' statistic. In June 1954, a report in the *Bristol Evening Post* was headed: "Drivers: Take Special Care On Estates", and continues:

> The City Coroner (Mr. J. Seymour Williams) urged at a Bristol inquest that drivers and people in charge of children should take special care on the new estates. "This is the seventh case." he said, "of an accident involving a child under two living on a housing estate that I have had to deal with in two years. This is a very serious state of affairs." The jury returned a verdict of "Accidental death" on Lynn Daly, aged 17 months of Greenditch Avenue, who was in collision with an ice-cream van. The father, Michael Joseph Daly, said the van stopped near his home and his wife went out and brought some ice-cream. When the van had moved off his wife found her son lying in the middle of the road.[173]

Moving into 1956, optimism rises again that the community centre will soon be built. In a slightly surreal snippet, the *Bristol Evening Post* reported:

> Students from the musical comedy town of Heidelberg ("the Student Prince") will be among a party of 30 due to visit Hartcliffe later this year to lend a hand with the erection of the

172 *Bristol Evening Post*, 21 November 1955.
173 *Bristol Evening Post*, 22 June 1954.

proposed community centre there. Work should commence in April, and volunteers should give their names to Mr. David Hope, 11 Moxham Drive, or Mr. J. Dix, 42 Gibbsfold Road.[174]

There is no report of the centre being started in April but reports of the Heidelberg visit continued:

One of the first tasks to be tackled by students from Oxford and Heidelberg universities when they arrive at Hartcliffe on Saturday for their three-week work camp will be to dig the gardens of 30 elderly and disabled people. The camp is organised by the Student Christian movement and its main job will be to help in building Hartcliffe's new community centre. Residents on the estate are providing accommodation and meals.[175]

A letter in September from David Hope, ex-chairman, Hartcliffe Community Association, does confirm that work has started on site, but vandalism hit the project:

The Hartcliffe Community Association is building its own centre and the two site huts on the Hareclive Road building site are the property of the Community Association by virtue of gift. Damage of the malicious type which has occurred in the past two weeks has caused considerable financial loss, but, equally important is the sense of frustration which might develop among the voluntary builders. The latest damage was not done by children.[176]

Another January, another AGM. "The financial situation at Hartcliffe is good. Although £150 was paid by the association as a first instalment on its new building, treasurer Mr B. G. Luffman reported a balance in hand of £58 13s. 7d. at the annual meeting".[177]

In February, Bristol city council formally agreed to lease half an acre of land to the community association for a nominal rent of £1 per year for 14 years.[178] This was a far smaller site than the original plan and

174 *Bristol Evening Post*, 2 March 1956.
175 *Bristol Evening Post*, 30 August 1956.
176 *Bristol Evening Post*, 4 September 1956.
177 *Bristol Evening Post*, 1 February 1957.
178 Council minutes, 12 February 1957, Bristol Archives.

it is clear that the land designated for a community garden and outdoor sports facilities were excluded from the lease.

On 10th May 1957, Hartcliffe experienced its first royal visit: Princess Margaret was given a tour of the estate and met the community association Chairman, Ray Sharland, who would go on to be the first community warden on the estate and would later be involved in founding the community farm. Later that year, he was also elected to the Bristol Federation of Community Groups. In 1995, I managed to get a street named in his honour when one was created as part of a regeneration project on the estate.

Into 1958 and Ray Sharland is reported as sending a warning to the people of the estate that the community association may disband. One can only assume that this was more of a call to action than a serious proposal to close but it was taken seriously by the local media:

Yet another community association has sounded the alarm to its members. This time it is Hartcliffe which faces disbandment. "Owing to a shortage of active committee members the association is in danger of disbanding," the chairman, Mr Ray Sharland has written in a circular to the people of Hartcliffe. This lack of committee members has meant a shortage of collectors, which in turn has led to a falling off in association membership and poor contact between the C.A. and those who have joined it. It is more than four years ago that Hartcliffe C.A. was formed. Its aims to provide social and educational facilities for everyone living on the estate, and to look after members' interests in general with regard to amenities there. Two years ago work began on a centre, but progress has been slow, once again because of the lack of volunteers. Now, with the annual general meeting on January 30 comes the appeal. "Unless we get a full measure of support at this meeting and a full working committee is formed, the outlook for this association is very dark," says Mr. Sharland. If the association is forced to disband it will mean Hartcliffe losing the chance of a community centre of its own—and losing the money paid in for the building. "I realise," he continues, "that a number of mistakes have been made in the past … now is the time in this New Year to look ahead. Please rally round and support your own association. We desperately need your help".[179]

179 *Bristol Evening Post*, 17 January 1958.

All was not lost as the scare tactics worked.

> Hartcliffe Association, which only recently was in danger of collapsing through lack of support, has received a much-needed 'shot in the arm' and is once more alive and kicking. At the recent annual meeting 74 people—all alarmed at the thoughts of a shut-down, struggled through the fog, and a full committee under the chairmanship of Mr R. Sharland was formed ... There weren't many offers to act as collectors and this problem is to be reviewed, together with the possibility of a regular broadsheet to keep members informed of association activities.[180]

The good news was soon tempered when the new building was hit once again:

> Hooligans removed the heavy planking covering the new drains, set in their concrete beds, and systematically smashed the clay pipes while the concrete was still wet. Not content with that, they smashed drain covers as well. A spokesman for the association told me: "This is not the work of children. They would not have the strength to lift the planking." Residents on the estate are asking themselves: "What is the point of going on? The centre has been a target for wanton damage ever since a start was made. Are the hooligans going to be less ferocious when it is completed?" I was told: "It must be the work of a teenage gang. Somebody must see them or know them. If we can't beat them now, there is no point in going on".[181]

The volunteers kept soldiering on though:

> In spite of all the setbacks, a small band of volunteers toll on. "We could do with some assistance. We should like to get as much done before the bad weather as possible." said one. When the vandals see the walls rising, they may let these premises alone. After all, they will benefit most by the completed centre. It seems senseless to break it up![182]

180 *Bristol Evening Post*, 7 February 1958.
181 *Bristol Evening Post*, 8 June 1958.
182 *Bristol Evening Post*, 25 July 1958.

Into the autumn and we find the community association in crisis once again.

> What is the future of the Hartcliffe C.A.? Concern is being expressed by members of the committee about the lack of interest in the association's affairs. Since former chairman, Ray Sharland, accepted a scholarship offered by the National Federation of Community Associations for a six-month course to qualify as a paid warden of a community centre, the association has been under the chairmanship of former treasurer, Mr. B. Luffman. To meet criticisms that the association are no longer contributing to the life of the estate, and in an effort to arouse fresh interest in their affairs. Mr. Luffman has decided that a committee meeting planned for next Wednesday shall become an open meeting".[183]

This doesn't appear to have produced the results as, in the new year, Mr Luffman continued with the same message. Speaking in advance of the AGM he says:

> For the association, as a group of community-minded citizens, the year has not been the success it could have been. Social events have been poorly attended, the only exception being the flower show, which achieved widespread acclamation and support. It seems fairly certain the lack of general support for our association is due neither to the type of activity offered, nor any flagging of interest on the part of committee members. In other words, we have no obvious cause for our failures during the last year. The first object of the new committee must, therefore, be to consider general policy and not simply to repeat last year's programme.[184]

Here we can pick up Derek Palmer's narrative again:

> When I arrived, it seemed to me that the choice before the churches was fairly simple. Either they had to develop their own social life, or they had to put their backs into reviving

---

183 *Bristol Evening Post*, 24 October 1958.
184 *Bristol Evening Post*, 23 January 1959.

the Community Association. We decided on the second course and within a few weeks of doing so we were informed that for financial reasons the University Settlement would have to withdraw its social worker. This was a terrible blow and one that we felt must be resisted. So in the autumn of 1959 the churches acted as a catalyst in a fusion of these three bodies [The Churches, the CA and the Advisory Council] into one to be known as Hartcliffe Community House. The House was to be under the control of a residents' association, but provision was made for six professional workers to be elected yearly to the Management Committee. This association also undertook to employ not only a full-time social worker but also a full-time warden. This was a great act of faith on behalf of everyone as there was no money and no building. The house began in a caravan and lived from day to day in the matter of finance. Bristol City Council agreed to help us erect a prefabricated building but it was not their policy as yet to have paid wardens.[185]

The idea of a prefab building was first raised through the Advisory Panel in the Spring at a meeting which mainly concerned undertaking a survey of local residents to gain an understanding of their needs.[186]

A major step forward came in the summer. The *Bristol Evening Post* reported a change in council policy:

In the past, Community Associations, backed by financial aid from the Education Committee have had to build their centres by voluntary labour. Now Hartcliffe have been told that they can erect a prefabricated building on the already constructed foundations in Hareclive Road. And that should mean the association will be in their own home by August or September. The only condition laid down by the Education Committee is that the foundations and site must be completely ready to receive the timber prefabricated first stage by August. The first stage, costing about £1,800, will include a small hall and kitchen and cloakroom. The Education Committee will pay 75 per cent of the cost and the association, who have about £500 in their building fund will meet the remainder. It is not yet

185 Palmer, Derek, *All Things New*, Star Books, 1963. p.104
186 *Bristol Evening Post*, 17 April 1959.

known when the second and third stages—another set of small rooms and a main hall—will be built. About £800 has already been spent since work started on the site in 1956. But interest in the project waned and work came almost to a standstill. Now enthusiasm is rising and officials are confident that their voluntary labour force will have the site ready by August.[187]

The establishment of the new combined organisation was announced in September by the chair of the Advisory Panel to an organisation called the Bristol Round Table. It is worth noting that the stigma which became associated with council estates is challenged at the very beginning of the speech, showing how ingrained this already was in the 1950s:

He spoke favourably of the estate and said that it was "jolly healthy" and "the accommodation was good." People tended to regard housing estates with suspicion, but it was only a very small number of residents which gave them a bad name. Dr. Leonard [a local GP] outlined a plan residents of Hartcliffe were hoping to put into operation in October. A new organisation Hartcliffe Community House an amalgamation of two other social bodies, the Community Association for Residents and the Hartcliffe Advisory Council, will go into operation from that date. The house will bring under one roof all the work which is being done on the estate and will act as a forum for local affairs.[188]

Good news followed quickly:

After only 14 days' existence Hartcliffe Community House is already proving its worth. Run at the moment from a caravan on the site in Hareclive Road, Community House has attracted a lot of attention from people on the estate with its population of about 15,000. Warden Mr. Ray Sharland—he is Bristol's first full-time official—is at present visiting organisations on the estate to interest them in affiliation and has already enrolled a number of members. He has started a dressmaking class and

187 *Bristol Evening Post*, 5 June 1959.
188 *Bristol Evening Post*, 30 September 1959.

plans soon to introduce a gardening class. Most activities must wait until the prefabricated building which will form the first stage of Community House is erected early next year. There is room for further development, but the policy of the House is to concentrate on staff rather than additional meeting space.[189]

This shows the completion of the building slipping again from autumn 1959 to 1960.

As the year was reaching the end, progress on the building was strong, "The walls are up and only the roof remains to be placed in position before members of the Community House turn their attention to the inside ... First to move into the new building will be warden, Mr Ray Sharland, who is now occupying a caravan next to the site. Offices for himself and for a social worker are included in the design. There will also be a kitchen, a committee room—to be used as general office during the day—and a small hall. "We are hoping this room will be used as a sort of meeting place where people will come for a chat and a cup of tea," says Mr. Sharland. "When things are running smoothly, we would like to see women volunteers running a tea bar each day on a rota system".[190]

The centre did open in 1960—seven years after the community association was formed to create it. The total cost had been £4,000 and it opened carrying a debt of £360. Once established, the centre proved successful with a further extension in 1968.[191]

The important factor was the council changing its policy that such buildings should be built by community volunteers. Following that change the centre was opened within less than a year. Given the original plans for the area and the influx of large numbers of people from across the city into Hartcliffe, surely the council could have turbocharged the creation of the community focus and the hosting of community activities if it had built the centre included in the plans at the same time as the homes were built. The expectation that an evolving and isolated community should have built the centre themselves was unrealistic and almost led to the implosion of the embryonic community association.

189 *Bristol Evening Post*, 14 October 1959.
190 *Bristol Evening Post*, 10 December 1959.
191 *At Home on the Slopes*, ACTA, 2002. p.46.

Churches

The development of churches on the estate would be much less problematic. This is because churches are part of well-established organisations with access to resources and the experience of providing buildings across the country. Land was reserved, as with the community centre, for three churches.

The first media mention of the need for provision came in 1952 from a report on the bishop's proposals to reorganise the diocese, "New buildings were mentioned in the report of the Bishop's Appeal Fund in which the urgent need for buildings on estates at Henbury and Hartcliffe was stressed".[192]

In the meantime, the Church of England was relying on people getting to the works canteen of a house building company and to nearby Bishopsworth:

There is good news about church activities on the Hartcliffe estate which are being run from St Peter's, Bishopsworth. The Sunday school, which is held in John Laing's men's canteen, Hareclive Road, is increasing its membership every week. Services are held in the canteen each Sunday evening.[193]

In the summer of 1953, the Church of England unveiled its plans:

At Hartcliffe, a church is to be built to a design which has never before been attempted in Bristol. It will be a modern structure to be built a stage at a time. The first stage will involve building a portion of the parish hall and a portion of the church at the same time ... The first part of the church will seat 160 people and the hall 200. Work will start before the end of the year if a licence can be obtained. The initial cost will be £12,000. The second stage of work will provide for a Sanctuary to be built on the church. Both portions of the building can be brought into full use in the first stage of the project. Hartcliffe will have its own priest.[194]

The report gave no indication when this building would open.

192 *Bristol Evening Post*, 21 May 1952.
193 *Bristol Evening Post*, 4 April 1953.
194 *Bristol Evening Post*, 15 August 1953.

In the autumn of 1954, the Bristol Diocese was ready to move forward with purchase of the site in Peterson Square, south of Symes Avenue:

If Bristol City Council approves the sale to the Bristol Diocese of a £2,500 site at Hartcliffe at its meeting next Tuesday, work on the church which will serve the estate will begin within the next few weeks. It is hoped to complete it before the end of next year. The building will be the first stage of what will eventually be the parish church. Hartcliffe is at present part of the parish of Bishopsworth, but long-term plans will probably provide for it to become a parish in its own right. Within the coming months it is hoped to announce a foundation stone-laying ceremony.[195]

The Methodists were also keen to be represented locally:

Leaders of British Methodism are watching with interest an experiment in church extension which is to be made on the new Hartcliffe area estate. For the first time a minister is to be placed on an estate as it is actually being built—only about half of the area's eventual population of 12,000 has so far taken up residence. Hitherto, the practice has been to send a minister to an estate when building is complete and it is possible to assess the religious needs and possibilities. Now Methodists feel that in the past valuable opportunities have been wasted by waiting and that a more energetic and enterprising approach is needed".[196]

John Taylor was appointed to the post and Rev Pope (a great name for a Methodist) commented:

Mr. Taylor will be there on the estate as it grows. We hope that the work of Christian witness will grow with the population. Our minister will be right in there in the middle of it all sharing the life of the people. We have found in the past that it is too late to send a minister when an estate is complete and the

195 *Bristol Evening Post*, 6 November 1954
196 *Bristol Evening Post*, 31 July 1954.

people are all there settled down into habits without a church or minister nearby.[197]

The article goes on to say:

When Mr. Taylor arrives on the estate he will be faced with the problem of starting Sunday services without a building in which to hold them. It will be more than two years before it is possible to erect a church hall. A site has been earmarked.[198]

Meanwhile, the Methodist Minister Rev Taylor was reported to be making an impact on the estate:

Already, the drive to foster the spiritual side of life on Hartcliffe estate has obtained encouraging results thanks to the pioneering work of the Rev. J Taylor. This minister-without-a-church has brought hundreds of people together in worship in his own council house at 46, Grinfield Road, and during services held in other council houses on the estate. The Sunday School alone attracts 170 children every week to Whitehouse School. Three separate meetings are held for women and the men have a discussion group. All that within nine months. Now plans have been drawn up to consolidate this progress with "an ambitious scheme for a church" and building is likely to start in a year's time.[199]

In 1955, the Catholic Church started to consider the needs of its worshippers, some of whom were travelling several miles to celebrate Mass:

The Hartcliffe estate will be the next district of Bristol in which Roman Catholic development will take place. Every week brings an increase in the Catholic population, and plans are being prepared to meet the needs of these people. At present the Catholics have no centre on the estate. The area is part of the parish of Holy Cross, Bedminster which is large and heavily populated. Worshippers have to go to Bedminster Down where

197 Ibid.
198 Ibid.
199 *Bristol Evening Post*, 21 Jan 1955.

for the past 20 years Mass has been said every Sunday morning in a pavilion, which is rented for a couple of hours a week. Other people at Hartcliffe attend services at Holy Cross, some travel into the city to St Mary's-on-the-Quay, while others go over to the Church of Christ the King, Filwood Park. Equal difficulties face parents in sending their children to Catholic schools. Holy Cross School is full and arrangements have been made for children to be taken by coach to St Mary's-on-the-Quay School in the city. The diocese plans to build both a church and a school at Hartcliffe. This is one of the most urgent projects facing the Bishop ... Already one of the priests spends much of his time on the estate, where there are 200 Catholic families, with new families arriving rapidly.[200]

In February 1955, 0.65 acres of land on Mowcroft Road was sold to the Methodist Church for £1,500, and, in March, 0.22 acres on Hareclive Road to the Catholic Church for £400.[201]

The first church to be completed was St Andrew's (C of E) which was dedicated on 18th May 1956. The *Bristol Post* was upbeat about the impact of the new building with its headline "Creating a living community".[202] It continued:

With the dedication of the new Parish Church of St. Andrew's at Hartcliffe tomorrow, one more step will have been taken in the slow process of converting a collection of houses into a living community ... The new church is surely one of the most modern in Bristol. Its glass façade and giant prefabricated concrete cross towering above the building are impressive. In spite of its modern appearance, the church has an air of quiet grace, beauty and dignity both outside and in. Because funds are low, and there is no immediate hope of a church hall, the church has to serve both recreation and worship. The interior of the building is divided into two by a special plaster board wall. One day there will be a hall, and then this special wall can easily be removed and the church used in a way for which it was originally planned. Inside, all is space and light. Enormous windows light up the two tall rooms. The

200 *Bristol Evening Post*, 22 January 1955.
201 Bristol Council Minutes, January & February 1955, Bristol Archives.
202 *Bristol Evening Post*, 17 May 1956.

blue and white decoration of the hall is a pleasant change from the usual drab colours and the interior of the church itself is breathtaking in its stark modern simplicity. There is a simple stone pulpit and font, a high red-panelled ceiling with sixteen blue stars and an altar wall made of prefabricated blocks carved with a deep grooved diamond pattern. Sapelle wood choir stalls; a simple wood screen in front of real organ pipes, and a pale blue and white mock organ pipes along the side of the instrument. It is a modern church in a modern setting to suit modern needs.[203]

At the dedication the Bishop emphasised that the church is not just a building:

> Do not start too quickly to try to get people to go to church, advised the Bishop of Bristol (Dr. F. A. Cockin), at the dedication last night of the church and hall of St Andrew's Hartcliffe. "To some the Church and its worship, the prayers and service that we use are quite strange and unfamiliar." Members of the congregation should enter fully into the ordinary life of the neighbourhood, bringing to it distinctive contributions of Christians. When people saw that church people shared to the full the things in which they were interested, some might say: "We might find something in this religion." Dr. Cockin said new housing centres offered the church what he thought was its greatest opportunity. The dedication of the church was a "very great occasion, but it takes much more than a building to make a church: from now on, it will be the task of the clergy and the lay people to do the real building—the bringing into being of a Christian community." At the service, the Bishop licensed the Rev. Ronald Armstrong as priest-in-charge of the conventional district of St. Andrew's ... Mr. E. J. Turnbull and Mr. M. Tippett, churchwardens, represented "the people" in the ceremonies.[204]

News of the new Catholic church hall followed a few days later:

---

203 Ibid.
204 *Bristol Evening Post*, 19 May 1956.

The opening of the new Roman Catholic Church at Hartcliffe estate, a contemporary, prefabricated building was described as "an occasion of very great satisfaction" by the Bishop of Clifton (the Rt. Rev. Joseph Rudderham) yesterday. The church, dedicated to St. Pius the Tenth, was filled for celebration of the first Mass. Dedicated privately last week, the new building will later become the church hall for a new Roman Catholic parish church to be built in the centre of the estate. "That church," said the Bishop, "will be the permanent parish church for this new and growing estate. It will be erected as soon as the opportunity arises. This is our temporary church".[205]

The Methodist church was completed in 1958:

Several obstacles and setbacks have been overcome at Hartcliffe, but at last the £40,000 building is complete. The church has pews for 250 people and room for a further 100 during special services. A church hall has a stage and seating accommodation for 350. About 150 can be housed in a lesser hall, and there is a four bedroom manse for the minister, the Rev. John Taylor, and his family ... the fact that a large part of the building cost has been met out of war-damage payments received for the Langton Street Church, Redcliffe, is to be commemorated with a tablet.[206]

Other religious sites were also allocated. In February 1958, land was allocated for a Pentecostal Church,[207] and, in June 1960, a site was also made available for the Salvation Army.[208]

Church of England vicar Derek Palmer became the first editor of a newspaper set up in 1959 by the local churches. In his book, *All Things New*, he gives the reasons for establishing the paper:

There is an urgent need in a new community for a method of spreading information, and while the local press can help in this it cannot do the whole job ... As a result of our thinking along these lines, four years ago the churches in Hartcliffe

205 *Bristol Evening Post*, 28 May 1956.
206 *Bristol Evening Post*, 3 May 1958.
207 Housing Committee Minutes, 24 February 1958, Bristol Archives.
208 Housing Committee Minutes, 13 June 1960, Bristol Archives.

decided to try a new experiment in church and community publicity and we are delighted that since then some other areas have worked on the same lines. Our basic concept was a parish newspaper, and not a church newspaper. This was not to be a church paper with odd items of local news thrown in to make weight, but a news service by and through the church for the whole community ... We therefore decided at the start that we must use newspaper format as for 90 per cent of our people this type of publication is the limit of their reading. We decided also that photographs and illustrations were essential if the lay-out was to be good and interesting each month. At the same time, we agreed that it should be entirely a joint affair belonging to both churches and that it should be run by them for the service of the whole community. The paper was to be called the *Hartcliffe Herald*...[209]

Youth services

The first discussions around establishing a youth club started in 1954. The *Bristol Evening Post* reported:

> The first big step towards giving the Hartcliffe estate a badly-needed youth club will be taken at Whitehouse Primary School, Fulford Road, next Thursday. It is hoped all prospective youth club members in the area will be present at the meeting ... The name selected for the new club is, not unnaturally, The Whitehouse Youth Club. It will cater for two age groups—the 10-14's and the 15 to 21's with a lively, attractive programme.[210]

This story is picked up again later in the month:

> The first meeting of the club called Whitehouse Youth Club, has been held and there is a move to get a grant towards building of a clubhouse. But members don't intend waiting for the builders to arrive if the club gets the grant. "We'll get down to the job after school and build it ourselves", a member proudly tells me.[211]

209 Palmer, Derek, *All Things New*, Star Books, 1963, p.106.
210 *Bristol Evening Post*, 12 June 1954.
211 *Bristol Evening Post*, 26 June 1954.

This self-build approach was clearly strong on the estate in the early days. As we have seen with the community association, it unfortunately gets in the way of buildings actually being completed. The initial response to the club is strong and within a month it had 225 members and was seeking access to "a piece of ground in Hareclive Road as a sports field".[212]

Later in 1954, discussions started with the council on building a purpose-built club, which could also possibly host classrooms and provide facilities for other groups including "old-age pensioners".[213] The lobbying was successful:

> Whitehouse Youth Club is looking for bricklayers, carpenters, electricians, plasterers and craftsmen of all descriptions, as well as a foreman to supervise the building of their new social centre on a one-acre site at the junction of Hareclive, Fulford and Hawkesfield Roads, near Pigeon House Farm. With a £4,000 grant from Bristol Education Committee, the club hopes to build a multi-purpose centre...[214]

The self-build approach did indeed lead to delays in getting the club built. The following Easter, it was reported that: "The problem of securing enough skilled and unskilled voluntary builders is causing officials to seek them OFF the estate".[215] This appeal is repeated again amid concerns for delays into the summer.[216]

A year went by without any progress and a fundraising carnival was arranged in the summer of 1956.

> Mr. Joe Hill, who is vice-president of the club ... has promised to give a "good slice" of the takings to the club for its building fund. The club which has 409 members, is at present meeting in Whitehouse School. It has been allocated a building site at Briscoe's Avenue and plans are now being prepared. There are hopes that the building will be complete by the end of the year.[217]

212 *Bristol Evening Post*, 1 July 1954.
213 *Bristol Evening Post*, 15 October 1954.
214 *Bristol Evening Post*, 26 November 1954.
215 *Bristol Evening Post*, 26 May 1955.
216 *Bristol Evening Post*, 8 July 1955.
217 *Bristol Evening Post*, 9 July 1956.

Swings in Hartcliffe Park (later renamed Willmott Park).

The centre finally opened in 1959 and was expanded in 1961. This was reported in the churches' community newspaper the *Hartcliffe Herald*:

> The club has been open for just over two years, but has already proved too small. In the past months the builders have doubled its size by building out on the far side. The great need was for smaller rooms so that more varied activities could be carried on. The club now has the most up-to-date Coffee Bar in Bristol and the layout and décor owes a great deal to the full-time leader Mr. Salmon. Beyond this there is a games room for table tennis and billiards and beyond that again a room that can be divided to make a library and a quiet room.[218]

Meanwhile, the Federation of Boys' Clubs was also developing a centre on the estate:

218 *Hartcliffe Herald*, April 1961.

At Murford Avenue, progress has been so good on the new Hartcliffe Boys Club building that it may be finished in October instead of December as was originally thought. The walls are up and the roof is going on. Meanwhile the Federation headquarters has not been slow to set about forming a management committee and appointing a leader … The club will be opened to fill an urgent need as soon as the building is ready.[219]

The club was finished in November, when it was reported:

Mr. Ernie Curtis is preparing for an invasion at Hartcliffe's new £13,000 boys club in Murford Avenue next Wednesday and Thursday. The invaders? Boys. For this is the week the estate has been waiting for; the week which marks the climax of the greatest ever building project of Bristol Federation of Boys' Clubs. The club is at last ready to receive its first members, and any youth between 13 years nine months and 18 years is welcome to enrol … As leader Mr. Curtis is anxious to get to know the boys personally, so he will admit only 30 to 40 for the club's opening on Monday week. The numbers will gradually be increased reaching their maximum of about 300 early in the New Year.[220]

In 1958, land on the Whitehouse Youth Club site was allocated for the building of a centre for the 12th Bristol (1st Hartcliffe) Cubs and Scouts:

Originally the group were allocated a site in the Englishcombe Road area. They felt this to be unsuitable in view of the long distance young cubs would have to walk on dark winter nights. A search of the estate provided several suitable alternatives and the Education Committee have approved the allocation of a piece of land in Briscoes Avenue at the rear of the White House Youth Club site. The lads are already busy raising money for their headquarters. One way is by collecting old jam jars. If enthusiasm is anything to go by, it won't be too long before they have their own roof over their heads.[221]

219 *Bristol Evening Post*, 7 July 1956.
220 *Bristol Evening Post*, 24 Nov 1956.
221 *Bristol Evening Post*, 8 August 1958.

Englishcombe Road is on the south of the estate and leads onto the undeveloped hinterlands of Dundry Hill. This location was identified for a Scout hut in the original plan for the estate, to give access to the countryside. The site chosen was in the heart of the estate and also the flatter area below the slopes of the hill, meaning going to the hut did not require an uphill walk for the Cubs and Scouts. While the fundraising for the hut continued, the Scouts, Guides and Boys' Brigade were based in the remaining Pottery Farm house in Grinfield Avenue. Distressingly this ended when a fire destroyed the building and required its smouldering remains to be demolished; St Andrew's Church came to the rescue and the activities were relocated in the parish hall.[222]

Later, the church built a hut on the church land for the Boy's Brigade.[223]

222 *Western Daily Press*, 1 March 1963.
223 Private correspondence held in the Bristol Archives from St Andrew's Church, 1963.

6. Retail, education and other infrastructure

Shops

The first residents moving into Hartcliffe found that there were no shops, so they had to trudge over the fields to Bishopsworth to use the small shops there, or rely on mobile shops, or catch a bus, again from Bishopsworth, to get further into the city. The original plan identified 20 shops in the main shopping centre, then groups of six in three locations dotted around the neighbourhood. However, before finalSising the retail plans, the council brought in a firm of consultants, Healey and Baker, whose report was submitted to the council in the summer of 1950:

> We have found Dundry to possess certain peculiar features which will have a great bearing on the siting of the shops; the contours of the land do not lend themselves to easy development and the natural features running through the Estate tend to split the layout into several distinct blocs. There is no absolutely level shopping plot near the topographical centre of the Estate, therefore, the Corporation will have to budget for a higher cost per unit than would normally be the case.

> In addition, the Corporation plans for the development of the Bishopsworth C.P.O. Zone [Withywood] should really be taken into account, and we are not altogether certain that Dundry should be regarded as a distinct and separate development, although for the purpose of this report we are acting on your instructions and assuming that both Estates are to be treated as separate entities.

> We have ... formed the conclusion that the few scattered shops in Bishopsworth Village and at Whitchurch will not attract any of the Dundry residents, therefore, it can be safely assumed that all the Corporations' tenants will do their daily shopping within the confines of the Estate. On the assumption that the area will ultimately contain no fewer than 3,130 dwellings, we have reached the conclusion that provision should be made in the Estate for a total of no more than 45 shopping units, i.e. approximately 850/900 feet of trading frontage. This allocation

should be deemed to be sufficient to provide for all different types of traders who will wish to be represented, private, multiple and Co-operative.

It is our recommendation that the main shopping centre should have an allocation of the equivalent of 30 "standard units", the remaining 15 being split up amongst the various subsidiary centres.[224]

This is a higher concentration of shops in the main centre, with fewer in the satellite ranks further out in the estate, as in the plan which received support only a few months earlier:

In our opinion you have already chosen the best location for the principal centre, it is roughly in the middle of the Estate and will be well served by Public Transport, and the ground levels … do not present an insuperable difficulty … your layout seems to run against the line of the contours, this of course will entail a successive stepping up along the terrace of shops. Shopping on a slope is not recommended apart altogether from the question of building costs, but it is a matter of opinion whether or not this is a better treatment than building parallel to the contour lines which in this case would necessitate excavating on one side of the terrace and building up the other.[225]

Scroll forward to 1954 and Symes Avenue has still not been completed but a retailer has been found:

Bristol Co-operative Society has provisionally agreed to take a lease of a site at Symes Avenue on the main shopping centre of the Hartcliffe Estate, for the erection of a multiple store with living accommodation over … The site extends to approximately 1,805 square yards, with a frontage of 125 feet, and the council is recommended, subject to the consent of the Minister of Housing and Local Government, to lease the site for a rental of £550 a year.[226]

224 Healey and Baker Report, 14 August 1950, Bristol Archives.
225 Ibid.
226 *Bristol Evening Post*, 7 October 1954.

Hartcliffe's first shops in Fulford Road.

Symes Avenue and the Co-op, with the locally named "Bishport Fives" tower blocks in the background.

The Co-op opened around 18 months later, also reported in the *Bristol Evening Post*:

Already more than 2,750 houses and flats are up and occupied. Shops are springing up at a number of points on the estate. To meet the needs of this growing "family", Bristol Co-operative Society opened a vast new emporium on Saturday—one of the largest stores of its kind in the country—and alongside, in Symes Avenue, more shops are well on the way to completion. The housewives of Hartcliffe will soon have no need to complain of the shopping facilities provided for them.[227]

Symes Avenue was finally up and running more than six years after it was planned and three long years after people started moving into this remote community.

Schools

The primary schools for Hartcliffe were originally given the imaginative names Hartcliffe Primary A, Hartcliffe Primary B and Hartcliffe Primary C. The council was aware of the need to get the first school built quickly to ensure that, when families moved in, the school was ready. The Education Committee was informed that the junior and infants' schools were included in the 1951/52 and 1952/53 building programmes.

Named after the nearby farm, Whitehouse (Hartcliffe A) was opened in time for the September 1953 school year, with an initial intake of 131 children and its full complement by the following April:

At the only new local school to be opened next term— Whitehouse Primary School, Hartcliffe Estate—the headmistress, Miss E. I. Herbert, and her staff will report for duty on Monday in order to meet the parents and children, who will be invited to look over the premises, which are at the moment only partly completed. This ultra-modern school, which for the present will accommodate 240 children is one of four designed to serve this new estate.[228]

---

227 *Bristol Evening Post*, 17 May 1956.
228 *Bristol Evening Post*, 28 August 1953.

Whitehouse School, Hartcliffe's first school.

Hartcliffe B followed two years later and named Hareclive School as it was directly across the main Hareclive Road from Whitehouse school. The Education sub-committee resolved: "As it is very near Whitehouse School it is recommended that it should be organised as a junior mixed and infants' school".[229] This school was built to provide places for 800 pupils.

However, the school would not be fully ready until the October of the school year, so that it was agreed that the five- and six-year-olds from both Hareclive and Whitehouse schools would attend the latter school on a half-time basis for the first month.

The same meeting was also told there was potentially a longer-term problem even after the completion of Hareclive School. The housing committee now proposed to increase the number of dwellings to 4,000 at Hartcliffe and 3,000 at Withywood, compared with the original plan for 2,800 and 2,000 respectively. This would require a corresponding increase in primary school provision. It was resolved that the numbers to be accommodated in the Withywood "B" school (Gay Elms) be increased from 560 to 800 and that an additional area be earmarked adjacent to the school, so as to allow for a future increase in its number of pupils should this prove necessary. It was also resolved:

229 Bristol Primary Education Sub-committee, 18 October 1954, Bristol Archives.

- that the Chief Education Officer be asked to discuss with the Roman Catholic authorities the question of increasing the size of the proposed Roman Catholic School;
- that the Ministry of Education be asked to agree the substitution of the first instalment of Withywood "B" School instead of Hartcliffe "C" in the 1956-57 building programme; the second instalment to follow in 1957-58, both being planned at the same time.[230]

One baffling issue here is that all council reports had previously indicated that in excess of 3,000 homes would be built in Hartcliffe and the number proposed originally was 3,100, not the 2,800 in the Chief Education Officer's report.

A further report returned the following month:

> The Chief Education Officer reported that he had, as requested at the last meeting, discussed with the Roman Catholic Authorities the question of increasing the size of the proposed Roman Catholic School at Withywood, which would serve children from Hartcliffe, Withywood, Highridge and Bishopsworth. The Development Plan provided for one school for 280 juniors and infants and a site of 4.25 acres had been reserved for the school, together with a church and presbytery. Owing to the increased number of dwellings now proposed for these estates, it had become clear that a school for 240 infants and 320 juniors would be needed, which would require 5 acres with a further .75 for the church and presbytery, and it was possible to increase the size of the present site to a little over 5 acres, subject to agreement by the Housing Committee.[231]

Unsurprisingly these changes were agreed. The item returned at the next meeting with another report from the Chief Education Officer:

> The report states that it is expected that there may, unless urgent action is taken, be an overall deficiency of about 1,200 primary school places in September 1957. The Chief Education Officer stated that he had approached the Ministry of Education to ask them to allow the inclusion of Hartcliffe C junior mixed

230 Ibid.
231 Primary Education Sub-committee, 17 October 1955, Bristol Archives.

Hareclive Primary School, 1958.

school in the 1956/57 programme; he also discussed with the City Architect the quickest way of securing the erection of Gay Elms School.[232]

There was some good news though: "Hareclive Infants' School opened on 3rd October, from which date all children resumed full-time attendance".[233]

The Ministry agreed to the changes to the programme provided the school could be started quickly enough.[234]

The next report in July was calmer and suggested everything was under control and "it was hoped to be able to keep pace with these rapidly growing estates and relief would be afforded by the temporary classroom provision at Whitehouse School".[235]

By the following January, the situation shifted once again. Now fewer homes were being built in Withywood but there were not enough school places in Hartcliffe. A process now started which would lead to

232 Primary Education Sub-committee, 14 November 1955, Bristol Archives.
233 Ibid.
234 Primary Education Sub-committee, 16 January 1956, Bristol Archives.
235 Primary Education Sub-committee, 16 July 1956, Bristol Archives.

regular tectonic shifting of the school catchment areas, with streets being moved in and out of school areas, particularly around the Hartcliffe/Withywood boundary. This must have been incredibly frustrating for the parents affected, as the Education department was juggling the school demand within the geography as new homes were built.[236]

In October 1957, Hartcliffe C school was finally named Teyfant.[237] The cost of building and equipping the school was £163,920 and was to accommodate 800 pupils, 320 infants and 480 juniors.[238]

In 1959 the council started to concern itself with what were then called ESN children:

...the Special Services Committee ... [recommended] that two classes for educationally sub-normal junior age children be established in the Hartcliffe and Withywood area in September 1959. The Chief Education Officer reported it would be possible to accommodate the classes in the main buildings of Whitehouse School provided an existing class could be accommodated in the premises of the Whitehouse Youth Club in Briscoe's Avenue.[239]

Even once all three primary schools were open, the provision did not meet the need. Temporary classrooms were constructed in the school playgrounds to accommodate the large number of children living on the estate. When I started at Hareclive school in the 1970s, those temporary classrooms still remained.

Tragedy struck on 8th January 1974 when high winds removed one of the roofs on a temporary building at Teyfant School. The roof was lifted and debris was thrown around, killing one child, Christopher Hollier, and injuring two others. Temporary supposedly, safe no.[240]

Of course, the later coroner's inquest decided that no-one was to blame despite the evidence suggesting that the building was not properly assembled.

Mr Kenneth Ford, scientific officer at the South West Forensic Laboratory, said tests proved that the bolts had not been fitted

---

236 Primary Education Sub-committee, 21 January 1957, Bristol Archives.
237 Primary Education Sub-committee, 21 October 1957, Bristol Archives.
238 Bristol City Council Minutes, 9 April 1957, Bristol Archives.
239 Primary Education Sub-committee, 16 February 1959, Bristol Archives.
240 *Bristol Evening Post*, 9 January 1974.

through the trusses into the stanchions of the building. The roof, he said would had to have been lifted 11 inches before the stanchions broke. Mr. Robert Wootton, senior scientific intelligence officer at the Forensic Science Laboratory said some of the brackets used had metal defects. Mr Wootton said these would have been caused by the bending or zinc covering process. The defects were not visible to the naked eye. Verdict: accident.[241]

This case achieved some national coverage and a report in *The Times* was more direct and detailed, the headline stated: "Classroom roof that blew off in gale had bolts missing, inquest on boy aged 10 is told", the article expanded on this:

Bolts were missing from a pre-fabricated classroom roof that disintegrated in a gale, an inquest in Bristol was told yesterday. Mr Frederick Pratten, chairman of F. Pratten and Co, of Midsomer Norton, Somerset, the company that built the classroom, said that even without the bolts it was possible for the roof to stay down on its own weight. The building would still comply with the standard code of design practice ... Mr Jack Fitten, whose carpentry company was subcontracted in the building of the classroom, said he had no record of which workers had worked on the project. The only possible excuse for the missing bolts was that the building stood up without them, and the workers would not have known to expect that of Pratten buildings.

Richard Clements, aged 10, of Hartcliffe, told the inquest that Christopher Hollier had been knocked down by flying debris after the class had been moved out of the building. Their teacher had decided to take them to the main school building when the plasterboard ceiling appeared insecure. "When I looked back I saw the roof of the classroom flapping. Then it came off and it was lifted up like a great kite", he said. "It was coming towards me so I crouched down and put my hands over my head. Then I saw a piece of the roof fly off and hit Christopher." ... The pre-fabricated classrooms had been used by Bristol

241 *Western Daily Press*, 9 March 1974.

Educational Authority for 25 years, Mr Daniel Dellaway, a Bristol Corporation technical officer, said. The one that that collapsed had been up for 10 years.[242]

There is so much that is shocking here, firstly that a building had not been properly constructed but no-one was held responsible, it was just declared an accident. Also concerning is that a temporary classroom was in place for ten years and it is possible that some were used for a quarter of a century. They probably continued to be used for years later. Meanwhile a young boy lay dead, "an accident."

The original plan promised six nursery schools. Ten years later none had been built. The council was informed in June 1959 that the Ministry had not approved the building of the first one.[243] The final provision of a specialist nursery school did not happen until the 1970s and only one was ever built.

Hartcliffe also needed a secondary school. This was in the original 1950 plan, and it was a rather sprawling low height building because of the restrictions set by the operation of the nearby Bristol Airport. However, a new airport opened on 1st May 1957 at Lulsgate in Somerset.[244] The restrictions were no longer necessary.

A 1956 plan for the school shows the configuration with the school on the Hawkfield Road/Bishport Avenue end of the site, where the original school was planned, plus the outline on Teyfant Road of a "Future Girls' School." The plan also shows the "Hartcliffe Primary School C" between the two secondary schools. The sports pavilion was no more, also removed were the café and the youth centre, although 14 acres on the east of the site was designated for "Youth Activities" and fenced off from the school playground. However, there was no building to support these activities and no indication what they would be. Interestingly this was also the first plan which showed a hospital site to the north of the school grounds.[245] This 1956 plan removed the public facilities on the site and also introduced a separate boys' and girls' school.

The budget for building the boys' school was set at £360,080 for the building, £36,050 for fees and £30,000 for equipment, a total of

---

242 *The Times*, 8 March 1974.
243 Primary Education Sub-committee, 15 June 1959 Bristol Archives.
244 *Bristol Evening Post*, 30 April 1957.
245 Hartcliffe Secondary School Plan, September 1956 (plus August 1958 fencing updates), Author's archive.

£426,130.[246] A council report reiterated the intentions set out in the plan: "This is the first of two schools each for 1,050 children planned to meet the needs of the Hartcliffe housing estate. Initially the first school will be for boys and girls but will become a boys' school when the second school, which will be for girls only, is built".[247]

It was not long before the school was caught up in political debate. In the May 1958 elections, the Citizen Party promoted their views on comprehensive education:

The policy of comprehensive schools puts Socialist theory before education. These schools are still only experimental, and we say that the nine of them already built are enough. There is much opposition to the building of more of them both inside and outside the teaching profession. It is only the Citizen Party who have clearly stated that they will do all in their power to keep the grammar school and technical school places open for the children of Bristol; nearly all of them free places. If the Socialists have their way, your child would be able to go to a grammar school only if you pay. The majority of the members of the Bristol Labour Party want to close these schools.[248]

In the same edition of the newspaper, the Labour Party was also given space for its views:

...the fear of the 11-plus examination has been lifted from parents and children living in the areas served by the comprehensive schools, and within a few years grammar and technical courses will be available for every boy and girl in Bristol who can profit by them during the whole of their period of secondary schooling.[249]

In the May 1958 local elections, the Citizen Party gained two seats, but still left Labour with a commanding majority of 22 on the council.[250] Once the elections were over, the debate shifted to the oak-panelled committee rooms of the Council House with the topic of the

246 Bristol City Council minutes, 9 April 1957.
247 Ibid.
248 Councillor Roy Berrill, *Bristol Evening Post*, 2 May 1958.
249 Councillor J Llewellyn, *Bristol Evening Post*, 2 May 1958.
250 *Bristol Evening Post*, 9 May 1958.

proposed Hartcliffe School at the centre of the battle. At the 'Special Sub-Committee of the Secondary Education Committee to consider matters affecting Secondary School Provision', the opposition Citizens' councillor Berrill moved the following motion:

> That, because the Comprehensive School is as yet only experimental and because the continued development of these schools to the exclusion of all others will inevitably lead to the closure of the Authority's grammar, technical and commercial schools, and will ultimately lead to the refusal by a Socialist controlled Authority to take free places at the direct grant schools, thereby removing from the majority of parents their fundamental freedom of choice, the development policy of the Authority should be to make secondary modern and grammar schools also available to all areas in accordance with the unanimous recommendation of the Teachers' Consultative Committee.[251]

If this proposal had been agreed, instead of Hartcliffe having a boys' and girls' school, it would have had a secondary modern and a grammar school. However, with such a large Labour majority this was never likely to happen. The Labour Party moved this counter motion:

> That the Sub-Committee, having carefully reviewed the progress of secondary education in Bristol since the war, have been most favourably impressed by the development of the new type of secondary school which is able to offer a variety of courses. The subcommittee recommend ... (2) that a similar type of secondary school be provided at Hartcliffe and Lawrence Weston respectively.

And by six votes to three, Hartcliffe School's future as comprehensive schools was fixed.[252]

The pressing need for the school to be completed was highlighted in the newly created *Hartcliffe Herald*:

---

251 Special Sub Committee, 17 June 1959, Bristol Archives.
252 Ibid.

The population here is rapidly growing and schools are filling up. Moreover, the bulge will soon be at secondary school age and the estate has not got such a school. What, many residents are asking, is the Bristol Education Committee doing about it? Dr Laybourn, the city's chief inspector of schools, supplied the answers. "By September this year the Teyfant junior school will be completed", he said. "We realise what an urgent need there soon will be on the estate for secondary education. That is why the school is going up in double-quick time." Work on it has just started. The main entrance will be in Bishport Avenue and cost £420,000. Like nearby Withywood School it will begin as a bi-lateral school and over the year will become a Comprehensive. But it is expected to be full by 1962 or 63 so another secondary school has yet been fixed but one education official predicted "probably within the next few years".[253]

This was followed up by the *Hartcliffe Herald* in the new year of the new decade:

The New Year does not only bring a chance for growth but for change also. The biggest change is that our children are growing up—the gaunt framework of Hartcliffe Secondary School which will be partly in use this September is an indication of this change. In a few years this school will be full and overflowing into a second school as our children enter their teens.[254]

In February 1960, *The Herald*[255] and the *Bristol Evening Post* both shared news that the new secondary school would open in Hareclive Road for the autumn term. Construction work was speeding ahead, so that September would see the first intake of approximately 300 eleven-year-old boys and girls arrive from Teyfant, Hareclive and Whitehouse Schools. The *Bristol Evening Post* also reported, however, that it would take a further year to complete work on the school, at an estimated cost of £322,000. Longer term, it was intended that the school would be for boys only, and that within four years a complementary school for girls would also be completed. The secondary school for boys was eventually

253 *The Hartcliffe Herald*, May 1959.
254 *The Hartcliffe Herald*, January 1960.
255 *The Hartcliffe Herald*, February 1960.

intended to be 'bi-lateral'[256], and to cater for 1,050 pupils from a larger area than the estate, entering on a selective basis. There were also plans to construct a new primary school on the border of Hartcliffe and Withywood.[257]

Writing in the *Hartcliffe Herald*, the new school's Headmaster, Mr Bradshaw, reflected:

> The new Secondary School opened in September in magnificent new buildings. A school, however, is much more than the building in which it is housed. The real thrill has been in the growth and welding into a new and living community of 260 children, their parents, 14 teachers, and the clerical, cleaning and canteen staff. We feel that everyone has been proud to be associated together with such a worthwhile task.[258]

As the focus switched to the building of the girls' school, a debate began about whether it was right to separate the sexes. In the summer, a campaign started to ditch the plans for separate schools for boys and girls and create a single large co-education school. At this time, in 1961, the control of the council had reversed with the Citizen Party now having a large majority and Cllr Berrill had become the Chairman of the Education Committee.

In June, the Education Committee reaffirmed its commitment to having gender-separated schools. The vote was divided on party lines, with Labour supporting a mixed school and the Citizens backing segregation.

> Chief Education Officer Mr. Harold Sylvester said single-sex schools were working well at Southmead, Filwood and Speedwell. The committee tried to give parents a choice by ringing the city with roughly alternating mixed and unmixed schools. Thus, close to the proposed unmixed schools at Hartcliffe there were mixed schools at Withywood and Hengrove. It was his department's experience that the maximum workable size for a school was about 1,500. Above this size staff became more tied up with administration than with teaching.

256 A bilateral school contains both grammar and non-selective streams, with the two groups of students taught separately.
257 *Bristol Evening Post*, 3 February 1960.
258 *The Hartcliffe Herald*, January 1961.

Mr. Sylvester said it would be difficult to recruit teachers for a school split horizontally into two by an age division. Every teacher liked to do some work in the upper part of the school. Citizen Party leader Cllr. Kenelm Dalby said some people apparently wanted the education authority to take over the roles also of church and parents. But the schools were only willing helpers in the social work of the other partners. Cllr. Norman Reece, the committee's vice-chairman, said if the committee decision was reversed delays in placing the contract for the second secondary school might be a year, causing a shortage of secondary places on the estate of 600-700. There would be close liaison between two single-sex schools, especially in sixth form work and school societies.[259]

The same paper carried a story of the activity and views on the estate:

Five thousand yellow leaflets have fluttered through the letter-boxes of Hartcliffe summoning all parents to tomorrow's decisive round in the estate's Battle of the Sexes. At a meeting in the estate's secondary school, they will be asked to back a petition to the Minister of Education against the Bristol Education Committee plan to segregate boys from girls into two single-sex Hartcliffe secondary schools. Clergy and social workers, backed by governors of the present co-educational school, are among those fighting the proposal to "unmix" children.

But the Education Committee insist that "education requirements" must have priority and are sticking to their guns. The fight is Hartcliffe's talking point today. And some of the anti-segregation group claim they have the support of the vast majority of parents. The group includes Mr W.A. Wilkins, M.P. three Bishopsworth councillors, the Rev. Derek Palmer, Vicar of Hartcliffe, and the Rev. John Earl, the Methodist minister, local practitioner Dr. Michael Leonard, and four social workers. If the campaign fails Hartcliffe will have a boys' secondary school and a girls' secondary school, each with 1,150 pupils. If it succeeds, there will be one mixed school of over 2,300 pupils.

259 *Bristol Evening Post*, 13 June 1961.

Success now depends entirely upon parents' support. "If the parents are against co-education, or if they are evenly divided at the meeting, or if they simply fail to turn up, we shall not feel strong enough to go to the Minister," said Mr. Palmer. But the vicar, himself a school governor and father of three children, is convinced co-education can and must continue. "I don't think the Education Committee are against co-education. The heart of the argument is the size of the school." He said, "We dislike intensely the division by sex, and feel that, to make the school manageable, some other division must be worked out.

"I feel myself that the whole school might be kept as one unit, with a division say, between the 11-14 year-olds and the senior children. One section could be run under its own deputy head teacher." Speaking as vicar, he went on: "I am very keen to foster the community. I feel that one school would come to be a tremendous unifying influence for the estate. "the size of the new school would not frighten us. Although no such school has been tried in Bristol before, it has been tried in London with success. It is quite obvious that in any school over 500 children the head teacher cannot have an intimate knowledge of every child. But a school of 2,000 has many educational advantages as well as its important social effect. "For instance, you can afford more specialist teachers. You can cater for minorities. You can have more equipment at your disposal."

What is the social importance of co-education? This was Mr. Palmer's view: "I am convinced the average child grows up to a more normal adulthood if he or she mixes the right way through education. All children are together up to the age of 11. Why then, just as they are beginning to become aware of their sex, should we pull them apart? I myself went to a boys' public school. I am sure I should have found it easier to accept the opposite sex later on had I been to a mixed secondary. Equally important, in mixed schools, boys and girls—some of whom may come from homes where there is strife between husband and wife—can see men and women on the staff working together quite normally."

Mr. Ray Sharland warden of Hartcliffe Community House, said he thought single-sex schools "socially undesirable." "They make an unnatural break when it is least wanted. Secondary school age becomes the only time in life now when the sexes are separated. Any disadvantages in a co-educational school are outweighed by the advantages".[260]

The *Evening Post* also talked to parents on the estate to gain an insight into views of those not directly involved in the campaign:

Said Mrs Olive Olden, mother of six children of 16, Kilmersdon Road: "I see no need for this violent opposition to the new plan. We have fallen over backwards in recent years to broaden our minds and teach children about sex and so on. I think segregation might be a good thing. I'm no Victorian. But we should give the Education Committee's proposal a fair trial." Mrs. Grace Edwards, of Witch Hazel Road, agreed. "I don't believe in co-education", she said, "and nobody can accuse me of being old fashioned. Put boys and girls together in a secondary school and their minds are not on their work. I go by results. My three daughters have been to a girls' school, and they have received a first class education. They didn't become shy about boys; on the other hand they haven't given me any of the 'dating' problems I think mixed schools produce."

Mrs. Joyce Comer, 42, Gatcombe Road, herself a manager of a local school said her experience had taught her the opposite. "My son goes to a co-educational school and takes girls for granted. My daughter went to a girls' school—when she left she had to overcome shyness with boys. I am sure 95 per cent of the people here want co-education. It is so much more natural. And quite the opposite of a distraction, the presence of the opposite sex becomes the accepted thing. By the time children are old enough to take interest in the opposite sex in a mixed school, they have got used to them being there."

Mrs. Betty Staynings, 6, Wroughton Gardens, mother of three, added: "Boys and girls should grow up together. I want my children to go to a mixed school."

260 Ibid.

And Mrs. Lillian Barrett, 28, Mowcroft Road, declared: "A co-educational school is the place for my daughter (11). I don't object to a big school. But I do object to separation. Boys and girls are happier together."

If the yellow leaflets have done their trick, the parents of Hartcliffe will battle it out tomorrow night. The organisers of the protest don't mind opposition—but they don't want apathy.[261]

Clearly there was not unanimity. Would people attend the meeting or would the largely empty hall just accommodate a few passionate people and many rows of empty chairs? The *Bristol Evening Post* story days later provides the answer:

Parents protested about the future of three schools in the Bristol area last night. At Hartcliffe they clamoured for co-education on the estate. By a five [sic] to one majority, parents decided to petition the Minister of Education (Sir David Eccles), in an attempt to reverse the present Education Committee plan for two single-sex schools. Voting was 115 for petitioning Sir David and 28 against.[262]

To get more than 140 people to a public meeting on the estate was an astounding feat and demonstrates the level of feeling on this issue in the area. The report continues:

Parents took part in discussion after hearing two opposing points of view … the chairman of the Education Committee, Cllr. Roy Berrill and the Chief Education Officer, Mr. Harold Sylvester put the official viewpoint. The Vicar of Hartcliffe (the Rev. Derek Palmer) spoke in favour of one large mixed school or two separate ones. Cllr. Berrill said the committee had decided on separate schools as a matter of principle. He said the start of the second school was immediate and plans were now being finalised. Any change would delay it by about a year.

261 Ibid.
262 *Bristol Evening Post*, 15 June 1961.

Mr Sylvester agreed that no-one was being arbitrary. The alternative to the present plan was a vast school of 2,400 pupils. This, he said, was not practicable. Bristol's biggest school was 1,500 and experience so far was that even that was a little too big. Two schools should not be thought of as distinct, out of touch. They could join in debating, plays, parent-teacher and old scholar associations and a school orchestra.

Mr Palmer said he spoke on behalf of the governors, as vicar, and as a parent of three children. The present secondary school was temporarily mixed. What a great shame that something which had started so wonderfully would be broken up. Another man said co-education would deprive Hartcliffe parents of the right of choice. He himself attended a co-education school— and was still scared of the opposite sex. One speaker said vandalism was often blamed on youngsters. That may well result from lack of discipline in school—which was why he favoured single sex schools. There was applause for a woman who said, "If parents have done their job properly, discipline from the teachers would come quite easily".[263]

The argument moved quickly to the letters page of the *Bristol Evening Post*. Under a headline "Our duty to refuse this plan" Cllr Berrill wrote:

The Education Committee of 38 members, after giving due consideration to the views put forward by Hartcliffe representatives have twice unanimously decided that a school of 2,400 is educationally wrong. It can be reasonably be expected, that, once established, two single sex schools will prove as popular and successful at Hartcliffe as they have been on another Bristol estate. Full consideration has and will in future be given to local wishes, but the committee have a duty to refuse to do something which they know to be wrong and not in the best interests of the children for whom they are responsible.[264]

The letter writing erupted in the Education Committee as Labour members saw the defence of small schools was an attack on

263 Ibid.
264 *Bristol Evening Post*, 21 June 1961.

the comprehensive system which tended to produce larger schools. Hartcliffe School was once again the focus of the council's debates on the wider issue of comprehensive education and its future was cemented into a party-political dispute.[265]

The campaign was not having an immediate effect, as even as late as September 1962 the reports of tendering for the school still describe it as a girls' school.[266] On the 27th, a tender to build the school was approved costing a total of £395,872.[267]

In May 1963, the campaign for co-education received a major boost as Labour regained control of the council. The final throw of the dice occurred on 26th September 1963.

> Mr Berrill moved … that bearing in mind all the circumstances, the committee adhere to their previous plan to provide two seven-form entry schools, one for boys and one for girls but closely related and integrated. After discussion, and on being put to the vote, this was not carried, sixteen members voting for the amendment and nineteen against … The adoption of Secondary Education Committee minute 544 was then moved, and on being put to the vote, this was declared carried, nineteen members voting for the adoption and sixteen members voting against.[268]

With that the issue was finally settled: the school would be mixed and it would be the largest school in Bristol with an East Building and a West Building. There was a legacy of the original intention, even when I went there as a pupil in 1974, as the technical workshops were in the West Building, and the cookery classes in the East Building, reflecting the mores of the 1950s.

Health

The original plan for Hartcliffe was to have a health centre on Hareclive Road on the opposite side to the community centre and a hundred yards further west. Prior to the health centre being built, across the estate, doctors' houses, or surgeries, were built with a consulting room

265 *Bristol Evening Post*, 30 June 1961.
266 *Bristol Evening Post*, 24 September 1962.
267 Bristol Education Committee, 27 September 1962, Bristol Archives.
268 Bristol Education Committee, 26 September 1963, Bristol Archives.

downstairs. They can be seen on the map of the estate produced by the housing department in the late 1950s, on Hawkfield Road, Hareclive Road, Hellier Walk, Bishport Avenue and Murford Avenue and they continued to function even after the clinic was built. A house was also reserved for a dentist, but it is not clear if it ever opened as one.[269]

In 1956, over three years after people had started moving into the area, the *Bristol Evening Post* reported on the development of the health clinic:

Nearing completion—it is to be opened in late June or early July—is an £11,000 health clinic. Its 32 rooms will provide all the main medical services—eyes, ears, nose, throat and teeth—and there are doctors' consulting rooms and pre- and anti-natal clinic rooms. One of the first things to be built, and one of the most important from the mothers' point of view, is the capacious pram shelter outside.[270]

Sadly, the new health centre was hit by the same problem as the community centre just across the road, vandalism:

Mr Rogers, managing director of W. Rogers and sons (Bristol), said: "We have built on every estate in Bristol and we have never encountered the damage we have found at Hartcliffe". "The effect of the damage has been to delay the completion of the clinic for two or three weeks, so the mothers and other residents of Hartcliffe will suffer. Everybody says it's Teddy boys, but I don't know whether it is or not. If this sort of thing is going to go on, we will not be able to take on any more jobs at Hartcliffe. They would simply not be economic".[271]

The Mary Hennessy Health Clinic was formally opened on 18th January 1957.[272]

Another key health building which didn't get built quite so quickly was the south Bristol hospital:

269 Hartcliffe Estate, Map, Bristol City Council, 1 July 1956, Author's Archive.
270 *Bristol Evening Post*, 17 May 1956.
271 *Bristol Evening Post*, 4 July 1956.
272 *Bristol Evening Post*, 19 January 1957.

Hartcliffe health centre named after Councillor Mary Hennessy.

The S.W. Regional Hospital Board had as far back as 1949 earmarked land at Petherton Road, Hengrove for the building of a hospital and Bristol Corporation had always envisaged the erection of a hospital there. But it is now clear that this site would be inadequate for a hospital to meet today's needs. The board is now hoping to get part of the airport site in view of the declared urgency for a hospital for Bristol South.[273]

This proposal resurfaced the following year when the airport closed:

The South West Regional Hospital Board, which at present holds a site of about 10½ acres in Wells Road, is prepared to release this to the corporation for the erection of a swimming bath and clinic, and will be given an alternative site for its proposed new hospital to serve South Bristol, on the airport.[274]

The campaign continued into the next decade:

273 *Bristol Evening Post*, 11 July 1955.
274 *Bristol Evening Post*, 19 May 1956.

The Lord Mayor of Bristol (Ald. Hugh Jenkins) last night emphasised the urgent need for a hospital in South Bristol, where about a third of the city's population live. He told members of the medical profession and the S.W. Regional Hospital Board that there were only two or three clinics south of the river on which people had to depend. In times of emergency in that part of the city the only access to hospital treatment was by crossing the river by bridges, and the existing bridges were too few and too narrow. "We have to have a hospital in South Bristol, and anything you can do to bring that dream and that requirement into something real will be something for which the people of South Bristol will bless you," he said.[275]

So 'urgent' was the 'dream' and 'requirement' that a hospital on the old airport land was not opened until 2012.

Pubs

The original plan included six pubs but when it came to allocating sites only four were accommodated: the Gatcombe House, the Fulford House, the Hartcliffe Inn and the Red Hart. It would be five years after people started moving into the area before pubs started to open. The nearest pubs until then were in Bishopsworth.

Built and owned by Bristol brewery, Georges & Co. Ltd,[276] the opening of the Hartcliffe Inn was announced in an advertorial in the *Bristol Evening Post* in December 1958:

The Hartcliffe Inn has come into being as a result of Georges' declared policy of post-war inn building to the latest and most comfortable design. Building, too, in places where the local housing programme has enlarged the city to an extent where the city drinker has to face a mile walk for a beer—or go without. Hartcliffe is one of the areas which for a long time has wanted something like the Hartcliffe Inn...[277]

275 *Bristol Evening Post*, 10 September 1960.
276 Georges became part of Courage in 1961.
277 *Bristol Evening Post*, 2 December 1958 (advertorial).

Under a headline "Two Public Houses Are Opening This Summer" the *Bristol Evening Post* 'reported' on the progress of pub building in Hartcliffe:

> Like a village, an estate community needs a public house. HARTCLIFFE is lucky; one new public house opened a few months ago and another two are already being built. The first pints will be pulled at Gatcombe House, Gatcombe Road, early in June; at Fulford House, Fulford Road, some time at the end of July. The brewery: Georges.[278]

The *Bristol Evening Post* continued with the promotional copy as the Gatcombe House was ready to open,

> The tenth new public house to be built since the Second World War by Messrs. Georges Bristol Brewery Ltd opens at Hartcliffe on Monday. It is the Gatcombe House, an inn which succeeds in combining the good points of an old English public house with the best of modern design. The façade, with its clean lines of Portland stone and cedarwood slatting, is essentially modern. So is the heating from beneath-the-floor electric wires. But there will be fires as well to fulfil a sociological and psychological purpose. In the public bar a long-mullioned window overlooks Horesham Grove, the chimney breast is of Portland stone, with a flower-alcove offsetting the hardness of the material.[279]

Unfortunately, the article did not expand on the sociological and psychological purpose.

An advert announcing the opening of the Fulford House was published in July 1959.[280]

The Red Hart followed a year later in 1960 and the *Bristol Evening Post* did not miss the opportunity for another glowing article. Reviewing the paper in that period, it is obvious the brewery was a substantial advertiser which probably helped with the coverage, and it is likely that the following article was a commissioned advertorial:

278 *Bristol Evening Post*, 20 March 1959.
279 *Bristol Evening Post*, 30 May 1959.
280 *Western Daily Press*, 28 July 1959 (advert).

The Red Hart, Hartcliffe, is to be opened today by Cllr. Chas O. Worth, Chairman of the Port of Bristol Authority, and it is of interest to note that Georges' connection with the Bristol Docks has exceeded 170 years. Records of shipping from Bristol show that the "Lovely Martha" took 32 casks of Georges' porter on November 29 1790 for shipment to Cork ... when a name was being sought for this new inn at Hartcliffe and bearing in mind the fact that the estate was itself named after "Hart Cliff"—an ancient field-name of the area [previous chapters show this to be really poor research]—it was decided to name it after the wild red deer rather than the creature of heraldry and mythology. Outside the inn a sign depicting a wild red hart of the kind that used to roam these uplands and such as are still to be found on Exmoor reminds the passer-by what our noblest creature of the wild looks like. This is the fourth licensed house to be built at Hartcliffe by the Georges Group and the 17th to be built in the environs of the city in the last 10 years.

This is a country-style pub, with steeply pitched and gabled roofs, dormer windows, white stucco walls and Cotswold stone...[281]

The only element missing was the sociological and psychological purpose.

Public transport

The first mention of Hartcliffe and buses was before anyone moved into the estate:

Bristol Housing Committee today approved an additional £700 towards the cost of transporting to Hartcliffe (Dundry) housing estate workmen engaged on road and sewer construction. Mr. T. Johnson, Deputy City Engineer (Housing), said there was a shortage of engineering labour, and it was obvious a man would not pay his own bus fare to get to Hartcliffe if he could get a job in the centre of the city.[282]

281 *Bristol Evening Post*, 5 December 1960 (possible advertorial).
282 *Bristol Evening Post*, 19 March 1951.

Waiting for the bus.

This snippet emphasises the remoteness of the estate. It appears no-one ever considered the reverse would also be true: that the cost of transport into the city and the employment centres would be a significant issue for the people who would later live on the estate.

In November 1953, the plan to extend a bus service into Hartcliffe caused concern in neighbouring areas:

> Residents of Chapel Road, Bishopsworth, already 'up in arms' at what they feel to be the chaos caused by the continuous stream of traffic right outside their front doors, are unhappy at the thought of a bus service being added.

> This fear resulted from the proposals by Bristol Tramways Company to extend the present bus route from Warmley to Bedminster Down so that it would serve the residents of Hartcliffe Estate.

> To reach the estate buses would have to pass through Whitchurch Lane and Chapel Road, which are narrow and

have house doors opening on to the road. There was no street lighting or footpaths.

"A chaotic death-trap" ... "A road where death lurks around every corner" ... "It is not safe to walk outside one's front door." These were a few of the remarks made by residents to a *Bristol Evening Post* reporter...

Mr. C. A. Wickham, a butcher in Chapel Road said with the added danger of buses it would not be long before someone was killed. "When building the Hartcliffe Estate the authorities were putting the cart before the horse. The estate was built and no thought was given of how the people were going to get in and out. A new road, I believe, is being built from the estate and this can be the only solution to the problem. Nobody should have been put there until there was available transport to get them in and out".[283]

Unfortunately, the reporter did not interview any residents of Hartcliffe or the Tramways company. However, it is clear from later reports that the service did go ahead despite the protests.

The following month the people of Hartcliffe were reported as giving the Tramways company a vote of thanks:

Hartcliffe residents are pleased with what the Tramways Company has been able to do. But they are anxious that last month's extension on route 8a should be only a start to a general improvement of bus services ... Mr F.W. Ford, tells me: "We would like to see a direct route to The Centre, an early-morning bus for Sunday workers, and some school buses for children attending the Southville and Ashton Gate schools".[284]

The knock-on effect of the growing number of Hartcliffe residents using buses was being felt further down the line in areas to the north of the estate such as Headley Park and Bedminster Down:

283 *Bristol Evening Post*, 13 Nov 1953.
284 *Bristol Evening Post*, 18 Dec 1953.

121

A deputation of four men and two women is to meet Bristol Tramways Co. representatives to press for a better bus service to Bedminster Down. They will tell company officials that they are: getting to work late and losing wages; missing the start of theatre shows; arriving in cinemas after films have begun; missing trains. All these inconveniences have been brought about—they contended last night ... because their number 8 bus was renamed 8A and extended out to Hartcliffe Estate. When Bristol-bound buses arrive at Bedminster Down from Hartcliffe there is no room for them to board, they claim ... Bristol Tramways introduced the 8A service last November on a temporary licence. They must apply next month to the SW Area Traffic Commissioners for a permanent licence ... Ald. Hennessy, who is one of the four council members on the General Passenger Transport Board said buses always had to be re-routed to cater for new estates. "You are experiencing now only part of the heavy drain on the existing services," he said.[285]

In May the story developed further, with plans to widen Whitchurch Lane to cope better with the traffic:

An immediate investigation is to be made by the Ministry of Transport and Civil Aviation into the problem of the Hartcliffe Estate bus service—which a Ministry ruling has put into jeopardy. A department of the Ministry, which handles the issuing of licences to public service vehicles, allowed Bristol Tramways Co. to run a service to the estate provided improvements were carried out to Whitchurch Lane, along which the buses run. Bristol Corporation produced a scheme, but another department of the Ministry declined to sanction the work because of shortage of money. Now Mr. W. A. Wilkins (M.P. for Bristol South) ... has secured a personal interview with Mr. Hugh Molson (Parliamentary Secretary to the Ministry) ... Mr Wilkins pointed out that there were around 3,500 or 4,000 people living on the estate, which was growing weekly, and the need for a bus service was getting greater than ever.[286]

285 *Bristol Evening Post*, 10 Feb 1954.
286 *Bristol Evening Post*, 29 May 1954.

In 1955, rumours started of an additional service to the estate:

Hartcliffe will have an additional bus service "during 1955" an official of Bristol Tramways Co. tells me but nothing more is definite. Plans are in hand to extend the No. 8 service which ends near Parson Street, Bedminster, terminating in Bishport Avenue, to serve the eastern side of the estate.[287]

This is an important change as it would bring buses into the estate using new roads rather than the pre-existing Whitchurch Lane. With the establishment of bus routes directly into the estate, the issue of public transport on the estate was to recede, limited to occasional letters to the *Bristol Evening Post*. Here are two of my favourites:

With the reference to the Headley Park residents' complaints of the bus service in that area, I together with many other Hartcliffe residents, am delighted that we shall be served by a bus through to Clifton. We shall not deeply regret if it is taken from Headley Park as a number of us remember when, about five years ago, Hartcliffe had no bus service, and we had to walk to Bishopsworth for any bus. We often used service 22 and residents of Headley Park treated us as though we had no business boarding their buses.

Hartcliffe resident with a memory.[288]

I thought when I moved to the Hartcliffe estate from Lawrence Weston some months ago, that I should be able to cut my travelling time in half. Alas, I had not made the acquaintance of the 6A bus service! Last Wednesday morning, I arrived at the Lampton Avenue, Hartcliffe bus stop and found 15 people there before me. Oh well, thought I, the conductor may be an ex-sardine packing factory hand and be able to get us all in. Ten minutes later an omnibus loaded over her Plimsoll line hove into view. Sailing past, it vanished into the murky horizon to the angry mutterings of the assembled queue, now numbering about 30 men and women hoping to be able to get to work in

287 *Bristol Evening Post*, 18 Mar 1955.
288 *Bristol Evening Post*, 13 June 1958.

time for the "lunch-break!" … The Omnibus Company say they are open to any suggestions. Here is one. Give the 16,000 people of Hartcliffe a six-minute bus service on the 6A, 6, and 22 services.

E. Iles.[289]

289 *Bristol Evening Post*, 14 December 1959.

Conclusion

The original intentions and plans for Hartcliffe were ambitious and laudable. Before it was built it was described as a new 'garden city', as it was being constructed and occupied it was described as an 'estate'. The chipping away at original neighbourhood aims and the failure to build facilities, or for them to come much later than intended, transformed a visionary project into a dormitory town. Early residents lived in an area without pavements, shops, community facilities, play areas, public transport, churches, or schools. To get to them they would have to traipse across muddy fields into neighbouring areas, where they were not always welcomed. It's hardly surprising that they were sometimes described at pioneers. As we can see from the record, many of the promised facilities were never built, many quietly and conveniently forgotten, with the land earmarked for them built over for more housing.

Hartcliffe was also affected by the change of government. It was planned by a Labour government committed to council housing and council estates to be for everyone but built under a Conservative government which saw home ownership as the main aspiration, with council housing as a last resort for the poor, or as a temporary steppingstone into home ownership.

Hartcliffe also suffered from its remoteness, not just that it was six miles away from the centre of the city but also that it wasn't on the way to anywhere, people only went there if they worked there or lived there. It was Bristol's largest cul-de-sac. The first people moving in felt isolated and ignored:

The people who take the decisions don't live up here. They don't know anything about it... *Alma Dolling.*[290]

You used to come up on the bus on Hartcliffe Way and you thought you were really coming out into the country.

It was the greatest mistake the corporation ever done when they just built houses, with no road, no facilities at all. There was no church, no shops. In those days it was so difficult to get a place. If you got a house, you just took it. *Jean Carey.*[291]

---

290   *Looking Back on Bristol, Hartcliffe People Remember*, Bristol Broadsides, 1978.
291   Ibid.

Sheila Horton (left) and Alma Dolling (right).

I know mother's doctor, when he came to see her when she was taken ill, he thought it was the back of beyond. Always used to say to her when she went to visit him, "Daughter still living out on the prairie?" *Sheila Horton.*[292]

My wife accepted the house before we knew properly where it was, not realising it was as far out of town. *S Gallimore.*[293]

Hartcliffe was not the only place in this situation. Across the country hundreds of 'peripheral estates' were built on the outskirts of towns and cities. There were also overspill estates and new towns. Indeed, Bristol built council housing in the surrounding areas which it had failed to subsume.

While the new towns benefited from a wider range of facilities, people in estates like Hartcliffe were expected to travel into the main town or city for entertainment and employment. There was no town hall acting as a civic focal point. Hartcliffe and estates like it were on the edge, out of sight and often out of mind.

292 Ibid.
293 *Remembering Hartcliffe, The First Twenty Years*, Hartcliffe History and Education Project 1996.

A major critique of the building of the estate was published in 1988 as part of a book looking at the city in the 1950s. Personally I think it is too harsh, exaggerated, even condescending and typical of an outsider view—the author is Michael Jenner, an architect—but it is worth considering:

The worst instance was the building of Hartcliffe ... Everywhere in Britain, the 1950s saw the planning of huge new estates whose designers learnt nothing from the lessons of the pre-war estates. Almost every big mistake which can be made in the design of a housing estate was made at Hartcliffe, and most of them had been made at Knowle West or elsewhere before the war. In the first place Hartcliffe is much too big. It has roughly the same population as Bridgwater, about 26,000 people, but with only a minute proportion of its facilities. 3 or 4 pubs instead of dozens, a few dozen shops instead of hundreds. Everybody who moved in was married with one or two children (or they didn't get the points to qualify), so all the adults and children were in roughly the same age brackets. When the now familiar problems of housewives' estate-induced loneliness and boredom appeared, there were soon hundreds of cases. The children all growing up together were packed into a single secondary school, which was the largest comprehensive in Bristol, a city of over-big comprehensives. When they reached the difficult years, they reached them together. What is almost as bad, though less mentioned nowadays, is that these estates were all one class. There were not only no grannies, with their remarkable calming and civilising effect, there were scarcely any middle-class people either: few people accustomed to giving a lead, who knew how to complain effectively, or how to get things done. In 1960, when the population was already 16,000, there were just six professionally qualified people living at Hartcliffe. I don't suppose the proportion is very different now, for who would choose to live there. It's miles from anywhere, and on no through routes. The few shops have a captive market, which usually means that prices are high and service poor. In the early days Hartcliffe people compared the dismal quality of their local shops with the eagerly competing service in the shops where they had grown up. As I have already said, when the 1950s estates were built, all existing features were bulldozed. To this day they are bleak and unlovely places. The design was worthy but dull and boring. They look what they were, places thrown up in a hurry.[294]

Some of this is reflected in Derek Palmer's book:

These estates are sometimes built on the 'neighbourhood unit' plan used in the new towns, but seldom to the same extent. Some estates are small enough to be units in themselves, but many others go up to 20,000 or 30,000 people in a single area. These cannot be self-contained areas as they are all dormitories for people who commute to a thousand firms all over the city. Very often shops, public houses and such simple things as phone boxes are in short supply. The large town is only four or five miles away—so why bother to risk building these things out on the estate? Both political parties claimed after the war that one-class estates would not be built, but in very few places has this worked out in practice. It is certainly true that post-war estates are a great improvement on pre-war ones and that they are only part filled from slum clearance areas, but both by age and by income the balance of the new estate in uneven.[295]

Bristol Forum, produced by a group of Bristol architects, found a positive view of the area from the local inhabitants, which is interesting as Jenner was on the editorial panel:

Despite all the drawbacks and mistakes, I found few who hated the place. I encountered feelings ranging from quiet contentment to real pride or criticisms of detail, nowhere did I hear sweeping condemnation. And there are people, though few of them, who are working with might and main to build the future now.[296]

The *Bristol Forum* article concludes by saying:

294   Michael Jenner, 'Alderman Hennessy's Bristol' in *Muddling Through: Bristol in the Fifties*, Redcliffe Press, 1988. p.26
295   Palmer, Derek, *All Things New*, Star Books, 1963. p.12.
296   Crofts, Tony, 'The Synthetic City' in *Bristol Forum 2*, May 1960, Bristol Forum Trust, Ken Stradling Collection.

The list of achievements is long if not unending. The difficulties are immense: the intractability of the estate as planned, the difficulty of getting an adequate body of local support, the lack of funds. In the long run, the fate of all these schemes rests on the people of Hartcliffe; and to date, they have shown themselves adaptable, hopeful and fairly willing to work. There is reason to hope that Hartcliffe will be the first of our synthetic towns to become a true community.[297]

As I have posted extracts and photographs from the estate onto social media, current and ex-residents have reflected on what a great place it was to grow up:

Fond memories of that house, we had fields over the back of us, our own playground. *BW.*

It was brilliant all that greenery and the animals. *CM.*

Our mothers would sit on the walls chatting while we played. Sweet memories. *TD.*

It was amazing to grow up here. We had our own mini town centre back in the day. *WH.*

My view is not that Hartcliffe's problem was that it was thrown up in a hurry, we can see it took many years to complete. I only found it bleak on a rainy day, in the sunshine it was a fantastic place to live; there was plenty of open space, hours of fun could be had in the stream, making dams, fishing (I only ever caught a fish once) jumping across the banks, walking into the countryside, Dundry Hill had some great tobogganing runs when the snow came.

The problem was that it was thrown up on the cheap. These days it would be called 'value engineering'. Cheap houses, cheap flats, everything was costed per house—for example the bridge that would add £8 per house. The powerful people were the accountants. Facilities in the plans disappeared, even from local memory. The barriers to providing others almost overwhelmed a community coming to terms with post-war austerity and being uprooted from across the city. We

297   Ibid.

have seen that key to building the community centre was removing the rule that it had to be built by voluntary labour.

In the media there are consistently three people who are selected as spokespeople for the area, Rev Derek Palmer and Dr Michael Leonard, both middle class voices living on the estate in accommodation tied to their jobs and, also, Ray Sharland who was a council tenant. Women's voices were only heard in 'vox pop' style interviews (although they are much more significantly represented in the 'memories' style publications).

It was an almost solely working-class area, which made it easier to ignore and side-line. As we have seen this was not accidental, but a direct result of Conservative government policy, something which commentators like Jenner fail to mention. Then it was also possible to denigrate and vilify. Even before it was built the people of Dundry did not want to be associated with a council estate.

The original plans for Hartcliffe were visionary: there was a dream for a better life after the war, a new beginning. Over the years, that vision was lost: Hartcliffe and the people who moved and grew up there were betrayed.

Appendices

Appendix 1: Hartcliffe timeline

12th January 1943   Bristol Council approves Housing Strategy.

13th August 1946   Bristol Council approves plan to build new housing on the Dundry Slopes and starts discussions of boundary extensions.

9th November 1946   Bristol Council agrees to seek boundary extension and formally adopts the neighbourhood model with three neighbourhood units earmarked for the Dundry Slopes.

July 1947   Bristol Council agrees to open discussions with Somerset County Council on the Dundry Slopes moving into Bristol.

November 1947   Bristol Council meets the national Boundary Commission to put its view on extending the City Boundary.

April 1948   Bristol Council applies to CPO farmland on Dundry Slopes.

5th May 1948   Bristol Council reports that Somerset County Council agree to Dundry Slopes moving into Bristol.

31st Dec 1948   Somerset Council write to Bristol expressing its concerns if housing were built on Dundry Slopes while still in Somerset.

January 1949   Inquiry into farm CPO takes place. Bristol Council is successful.

28th January 1949	Bristol Council receives report on the problems of having an estate built on the Dundry Slopes.
June 1949	The government winds up national Boundary Commission.
13th September 1949	Bristol Council approves Dundry Slopes moving into Bristol.
4th October 1949	Somerset Council approves Dundry Slopes moving into Bristol.
24th January 1950	Detailed plan for the new estate in approved by Bristol Council.
March 1950	The government refuses to fully fund dual carriageway road to the new development.
March 1950	Council decides to bury stream running through the middle of the estate to save costs of building bridges.
May 1950	Bristol Council approves single carriageway road to the new development.
14th August 1950	Consultants report on shopping in Hartcliffe approved by Bristol Council.
1st April 1951	Bristol boundary change formally finalized by the government.
10th May 1951	Citizen Party wins majority control of Bristol Council.
4th June 1951	Bristol Council selects name "New Dundry" for the neighbourhood.
4th June 1951	Bristol Council agrees to adopt reduced housing standards for new council housing.

19th June 1951	Dundry Parish objection to the new name is registered.
4th September 1951	Bristol Council selects name "Hartcliffe" for the area.
25th October 1951	Election of Conservative government.
28th May 1952	First contracts for new council houses in Hartcliffe approved.
Autumn 1952	First residents move into the estate.
	1st September 1953 Whitehouse School Opens.
October 1953	First petition on the estate (about mud and lack of proper roads and pavements).
November 1953	First bus service extended into Hartcliffe.
Winter 1953	Hartcliffe Community Association set up.
January 1954	Hartcliffe Community Association holds its first event.
January 1955	Hartcliffe Advisory Council set up.
July 1955	Whitchurch Airport site proposed as location for new south Bristol Hospital.
October 1955	Hareclive School opens.
19th November 1955	Planning Conference hosted on the estate.
12th May 1956	Co-operative store is first shop in Symes Avenue to open.
18th May 1956	St Andrew's Church (CoE) opened and dedicated.

26th May 1956	Catholic Church opened.
28th Nov 1956	Hartcliffe Boys' Club opens.
June 1956	Youth Centre starts operating at Whitehouse School.
18th January 1957	Hartcliffe Health Centre opens.
1st May 1957	Bristol airport relocated from Whitchurch to Lulsgate Bottom.
10th May 1957	Visit of Princess Margaret.
May 1958	Methodist Church opened.
December 1958	Hartcliffe Inn opened.
March 1959	Whitehouse Youth Club opens on Briscoes Avenue.
April 1959	First edition of the *Hartcliffe Herald*.
May 1959	Gatcombe House opens.
5th June 1959	Bristol Council drops policy that community buildings have to be constructed by voluntary labour.
July 1959	Fulford Inn opens.
September 1959	Some Whitehouse classes moved to the youth centre to accommodate special needs classes in the school.
September 1959	Teyfant School opens.
1st October 1959	Hartcliffe Community House set up.

1960	Hartcliffe Community Centre opens.
September 1960	Hartcliffe Secondary School opens.
5th December 1960	Red Hart opens.
June 1961	Campaign starts for Hartcliffe School to remain co-educational.
1963	Rev Palmer publishes his guidebook on setting up parishes on new estates which almost exclusively recounts his experiences in Hartcliffe.
26th September 1963	Bristol Council ditches plans for separate boys' and girls' secondary schools in Hartcliffe.
March 1974	Hartcliffe Library opens.

Appendix 2: Extracts from a Joint Meeting of the Housing and Planning and Reconstruction Committees, 28th January 1949

(source: Bristol Archives, 10048/1)

15. The Dundry Slopes Estate (which is almost entirely outside the City Boundary) must therefore be ready for use before the middle of 1950, if the Corporation is to maintain its present rate of output of houses.

16. The City Council made a Compulsory Purchase Order on 13th January 1948, in respect of the estate, but despite every effort by your officers it was not possible to get the site cleared by the various ministries and the date of the Inquiry fixed earlier than the 11th January, 1949.

17. A period of approximately three years elapses between the decision to acquire a site within the City Boundary of the size and nature of Dundry and house plots becoming available for building.

18. The layout and drainage of the Dundry Slopes site has become a matter of greatest urgency, particularly when it is remembered that the site is not within the City Boundary, and the control of planning and the contribution of all services is not vested in the one body, namely, the City Council.

19. Assuming the Dundry Compulsory Purchase Order is confirmed without modification, and also assuming that it is ready for building by the middle of 1950, it is estimated that the Estate will provide only sufficient sites until, say, the middle of 1951.

20. Under existing circumstances and conditions your officers are of the opinion that it is not wise to assume that housing estates outside the City can be ready within three years from the decision to acquire.

21. There are <u>now no large tracts of land available for housing estates within the City Boundary.</u> It is clear, therefore, that if the building programme of the City Council is to be kept at its present level, further land must be acquired <u>outside the City</u> and, of course, the decision to do this in the case of Dundry area has already been taken.

22. When the City Council decided upon the acquisition of the land at Dundry it was hoped that the recommendations of the Boundary Commission as to the extension of the City boundaries would be put into effect in the reasonably near future. At present the position is that the decisions of the Boundary Commission are complicated by their view that there is a need for an alteration not only in local government areas, but also in the structure of local government generally. This alteration would need legislation which will undoubtedly be controversial, and it is quite plain that it will not be settled during the lifetime of the present Parliament, unless a very big change comes quickly in the expressed intentions. It does not seem clear whether these intentions are government policy or the expressions of individual Ministerial opinions.

23. The position is further complicated by the fact that ... once altered the local government area the Commission cannot, except for special reasons, make another alteration in the area for a period of ten years. It therefore follows that any alteration to the boundaries between Bristol and Somerset, intended as an interim or temporary settlement, would ... block any further alteration for ten years, not only in the case of the Bristol-Somerset boundary, but also Bristol-Gloucestershire boundaries and the Somerset-Bath boundaries. The Boundary Commission, therefore, can do nothing to assist in present circumstances, neither can local authorities come to any effective agreement with regard to boundaries.

24. Representations have been made to the members of Parliament for the City, the Ministry of Health and to the Association of Municipal Corporations for the speedy removal of this particular obstacle.

25. Attention has been called to the lapse in time between the first proposals to acquire land and house plots becoming available for building, and whilst your Officers are making every endeavour to be ready with the Dundry site by the middle of 1950 no assurances can be given that it will be ready.

26. The Corporation will be putting outside the city children under 15 years of age and as the number of such children forms a factor in the calculation of the formula, on the Corporation's side, for assessing Exchequer equalisation Grant this will reduce their chances of obtaining

such Grant. The amount of Education Grant may also be affected ... The expenditure on the provision of these services by the County Authorities cannot be ascertained until the estimates ... are available, but it will undoubtedly be considerable.

27. It appears contrary to accepted notions of democratic local government that there should be a community approaching 10,000 Bristolians without any vote in the management of the housing estate on which they live except that of an ordinary tenant.

28. There are, of course, the strongest administrative reasons why the City boundaries should include any new housing estates provided by the City. The erection of housing estates necessarily involves the provision of public service.

29. The County Council will have to provide either itself or through the appropriate Rural District Council the following services –

(C.C.)	Police
	Public Halls
	Community Centres, etc
	Education
(R.D.C.)	Street lighting
	Refuse disposal
(C.C.)	Health services
	Welfare services
	Children's care
	Food and Drugs Inspection
(R.D.C.)	Take over and maintain the highways and services on the Estate
	The area is already covered for fire services by the City.

30. In return for providing the services referred to in paragraph 29 the County Council and the District Council will, of course, be entitled to

the rates from the properties, as it is for services such as these that rates are leviable.

31. The power in the Housing Act to erect dwelling houses outside a local authority's area includes power to execute works necessary or incidental to the carrying out of the housing operations … but this power is not intended to cover the provision of local government services as set out in paragraph 29.

32. There is no financial adjustment now on a city extension other than the payment for physical assets taken over, such as schools, police stations, libraries, etc.

33. The difficulties in paragraph 26 above in connection with the provision of schools would recur in a greater or less degree in connection with each of the services referred to in paragraph 29. The outside authorities will be involved in the provision of local government services over and above anything they have in mind for their own population, for people who are really the responsibility of Bristol. In the case of the services provided by the District Council the new estate will add very substantially to their responsibilities. The population of Long Ashton is about 22,000 so that the erection of houses at Dundry would increase the population of the Rural District by approaching 50 per cent. It will be remembered that the Dundry area is one which the Boundary Commission have recommended shall be transferred to Bristol, so that the situation will arise that local government services, schools, clinics, libraries, etc., will have to be provided by the appropriate local authority in the knowledge that the Boundary Commission has already recommended the transfer of the area to Bristol and that these recommendations might well be implemented. Similarly, the District Council might find that their administrative and technical staff would need increasing to deal with an increase in population which, though substantial, was not likely to be permanent. This view has been seen from a letter addressed by the Clerk of the Council to the Somerset members of Parliament.

34. There would obviously be a tendency to provide services on a temporary basis and there would be understandable reluctance to plan or think ahead or to administer on anything except a day to day basis.

36. The Officers have considered what other areas outside the City might be acquired for further development for housing purposes. Two areas suggest themselves, one in the Filton district and the other at Mangotsfield. In both the problems already enumerated for Dundry, the cost of which it is impossible to assess at the present time as no data are available. The capital expenditure involved, will, however, be very considerable.

37. All these considerations point to the conclusion that the house building programme of the City will inevitably come to an end unless large areas outside the City are acquired.

38. The only solution is the Boundary Extension already recommended by the Commission, and that solution is not likely to be implemented for some years.

39. In these circumstances, the officers feel that the City Council should be made aware of the impossible situation in which the City is placed, with a view to this matter being brought to the notice of the Members of Parliament and the Minister of Health. A letter calling attention to the difficulties ... has already been sent to the Members of Parliament and to the Minister.

40. The Committees will appreciate from the contents of this report that the housing policy of the City is now wrapped up with the question of Boundary Extension and the closest consultations between the Housing and Planning and Reconstruction Committees will be necessary in the future; it is therefore proposed to submit this report to both Committees.

41. Your Officers in preparing this report set out to place before the Committees the facts of the position but in doing so it has been necessary to draw attention to the absurdities of the situation in which the City and the County Council are placed.

Sources and Bibliography

Abercrombie P And Brueton, B, *Bristol & Bath Regional Planning Scheme* (London, Hodder & Stoughton, 1930)

ACTA Community Theatre, *At Home on the Slopes, A History of Hartcliffe and Withywood* (Bristol, ACTA Community Theatre, 2002)

Banton, A, *Bishopsworth, Withywood and Hartcliffe* (Stroud, Chalford Publishing Co. 1996)

Benn, T, Years of Hope, Diaries, Papers and Letters 1940 -1962 (London, Hutchinson, 1994)

Bild, I, *Looking Back on Bristol, Hartcliffe People Remember* (Bristol, Bristol Broadsides, 1979)

Boughton, J, *Municipal Dreams, The Rise and Fall of Council Housing* (London, Verso, 2018)

Bristol Broadsides, *The Bristol Picture Book Part Two. Twenty Years of People's lives in photographs 1940-1960* (Bristol, Bristol Broadsides, 1987)

Brooks, T and Messiah, M. *Memories of Hartcliffe* (Bristol, Dundry Pioneers Local History Group, 1999)

Estorick, E, *Stafford Cripps* (London, William Heinemann Ltd, 1949)

Foot, M, *Aneurin Bevan, A Biography, Volume Two: 1945-1960* (London, Davis-Poynter 1973)

Frys, *English City, The Story of Bristol*, (Bristol, J S Frys and Sons Ltd, 1945)

Hanley, L, *Estates an Intimate History* (London, Granta Books, 2007)

Harris,H.C.W, *Housing Nomenclature in Bristol* (Bristol, City and County of Bristol, 1969)

Hart, G. S. *Whitchurch Airport: An Account of the early Days of Flying in the Bristol Area* (Bristol, Crockerne Books, 1997)

Hunt, S, Yesterday's To-morrow, Bristol's Garden Suburbs (Bristol, Bristol Radical History Group, 2008)

Jenner, M, *Muddling Through, Bristol in the Fifties* (Bristol, Redcliffe Press, 1988)

Mee, A, The King's England, *Somerset* (London, Caxton Publishing Company, 1949)

Ministry of Health, Ministry of Works, *Housing Manual 1944* (London, H. M. Stationary Office , 1944)

Ministry of Housing and Local Government, *Postwar Housing in the United Kingdom* (London, H. M. Stationary Office, 1962)

Palmer, D,
New (London, Star Books, A.R. Mowbray & Co, 1963)

Punter, J. V, *Design Control in Bristol 1940-1999* (Bristol, Redcliffe Press, 1990)

Quaife, I, *Remembering Hartcliffe, The First Twenty Years* (Bristol, Hartcliffe History and Education Project and Bristol City Council, 1966)

Ravetz, A, *Council Housing and Culture, The History of a Social Experiment* (London, Routledge, 2001)

RIBA, *Rebuilding Britain* (London, Lund Humphries, 1943)

Smith, P, *Homes for Heroes 100, Council Estate Memories, Bristol* (Bristol, Bristol Cultural Development Partnership, 2019)

Tickell, J, *Turning Hopes into Homes, A Short History of Affordable Housing* (London, National Housing Federation, 1996)

Newspapers

Bristol Post
Hartcliffe Herald
The Times
Western Daily Press

Websites

BME National, "Our Roots" (www.bmenational.co.uk)
British Newspaper Archive (www.britishnewspaperarchive.co.uk)
Hansard (https://hansard.parliament.uk/)
Municipal Dreams (www.municipaldreams.wordpress.com)

Archives

Bristol Archives
Ken Stradling Collection

Film

The Way We Live, Jill Craigie, Two Cities Films, 1946

Picture credits

Page vi—© Historic England Archive. John Laing Photographic Collection.

Page 4—Hennessy: Bristol Archives 40826/COU/3/10/1. Gill: Bristol Archives 35510/Com/16/1/26.

Page 8—*Bristol Evening Post* 5 Nov 1946 Bristol Archives 43980/2.

Page 13—*English City, The Story of Bristol,* J S Fry and Sons Ltd, 1945.

Page 14— Bristol Archives 40826/HSG/144.

Page 19—*Bristol Evening Post* 8 April 1948 Bristol Archives 43980/2.

Page 20—*Bristol Evening Post* 8 Sept 1949 Bristol Archives 43980/2.

Page 36— Author's papers.

Page 39— Bristol Archives 40307/1/4.

Page 42—Bristol Archives 40826/HSG/56/2.

Page 44 top—Bristol Archives 40826/HSG/144.

Page 44 bottom—Bristol Archives 43980/2.

Page 49 top & bottom—*Bristol Forum**.

Page 54—*Bristol Forum**.

Page 56 top—Bristol Archives 40307/3/12/7.

Page 56 bottom—Bristol Archives 40307/2/22.

Page 58—*Bristol Evening Post* 10 Nov 1953.

Page 61—*Bristol Forum**.

Page 92—*Bristol Forum**.

Page 97 top—Bristol Archives 35510/Com/16/1/4.

Page 97 bottom—Bristol Archives 35510/Com/16/1/27.

Page 99—Courtesy of *Bristol Evening Post.*

Page 101—*The Bristol Picture Book Part 2,* courtesy Bristol Broadsides.

Page 116—*The Bristol Picture Book Part 2,* courtesy Bristol Broadsides.

Page 120—*Bristol Forum**.

Page 126—*Looking back on Bristol: Hartcliffe people remember,* Bristol Broadsides. Bristol Archives 44659/PM/6.

*Photographs by Derek Balmer published in the journal *Bristol Forum* 2. Reproduced by kind permission of Derek Balmer and the Ken Stradling Collection, 48 Park Row, Bristol, BS1 5LH. © Stradling Collection 2023.

Acknowledgements

The staff of the Bristol Archives and the Bristol Central Library.

The following readers: Andrew Kelly, Robin Fletcher and Kate Smith.

Those involved in organising the original presentation including, Tony Dyer, Kerry Bailes, Karen Marie, Gill Simmons, Anna Haydock-Wilson and Roger Ball.

People who gave me access to archives: Tanya Martin (Ken Stradling Collection) and Danielle Sinnett (UWE Built Environment).

Those who gave me helpful advice including Eugene Byrne, Ted Fowler, Mike Manson, John Boughton, Robin Fletcher, Tristan Cork, Neil Maggs and Nicola Bowden-Jones (for tolerating me going on about it all the time).

Thank you also to the volunteers of the Bristol Radical History Group who have dedicated an enormous amount of time to the editing, design and production of this publication.

To all the people of Hartcliffe who have put up with so much and got so little over the decades. In particular, all of those who have died before reaching their 60th birthday including my brother David who passed away aged 57 while I was writing this book.